Collected Memories

GEORGE L. MOSSE SERIES
IN MODERN EUROPEAN CULTURAL AND
INTELLECTUAL HISTORY

Collected Memories

Holocaust History and
Postwar Testimony

Christopher R. Browning

THE UNIVERSITY OF WISCONSIN PRESS

The University of Wisconsin Press
1930 Monroe Street
Madison, Wisconsin 53711

www.wisc.edu/wisconsinpress/

3 Henrietta Street
London WC2E 8LU, England

Copyright © 2003
The Board of Regents of the University of Wisconsin System
All rights reserved

1   3   5   4   2

Printed in the United States of America

Library of Congress Cataloging-in-Publication Data
Browning, Christopher R.
Collected memories : Holocaust history and postwar testimony /
Christopher R. Browning.
p.   cm.
(George L. Mosse series in modern European cultural and intellectual history)
Includes bibliographical references and index.
ISBN 0-299-18980-5 (hardcover: alk. paper)
ISBN 0-299-18984-8 (pbk.: alk. paper)
1. Holocaust, Jewish (1939–1945)—Historiography.
2. Holocaust, Jewish (1939–1945)—Personal narratives.   3. Memory.
4. Eichmann, Adolf, 1906–1962.   I. Title.   II. Series.
D804.348.B77   2004
940.53′18—dc21   2003007237

For those colleagues of George L. Mosse in the Department of History at the University of Wisconsin–Madison with whom I had the honor and privilege of pursuing my graduate studies

Robert Koehl
Edward Gargan
Theodore Hamerow
Maurice Meisner
John Dower

Contents

Preface

It is a tremendous honor to have been asked to return to the University of Wisconsin campus in Madison to deliver the first George L. Mosse Lectures. But I am also awed by the responsibility, for we all hope and expect that this biennial event will become an appropriate expression of our affection, respect, and gratitude for George and for all that he meant to his students, friends, and colleagues; to both the University of Wisconsin–Madison and his second academic home, the Hebrew University of Jerusalem; and to the historical profession at large.

George's friendship as well as his constant encouragement and support for my work from the very earliest stages of my career were to me a source of immense gratification. He was of course an overwhelmingly generous person in such matters, and there are countless others who are similarly indebted to him. But I had always been aware, and I became even more so after being invited to deliver these lectures, that the kinds of history that we wrote could not have been more different. George's scholarship spanned centuries as well as such enormous topics as nationalism, racism, and sexuality, to name but a few. In contrast, I have carried out microhistorical examinations of selected aspects of the Holocaust, confined to the brief span of a few years.

In regard to this anomaly, it is only fitting to relate a "George story" that I heard just recently. When the history department of a major university was conducting a search, George encouraged them to consider someone who had published a narrowly focused, densely researched, thoroughly empirical study of one relatively obscure but interesting institution in the Third Reich. A member of the department in question asked George in surprise why he was so supportive of someone whose work was so different from his own. George replied with his mischievous twinkle, "Those of us who survey the broad landscape still love the twigs and bushes." Thus I hope that it was not unfitting on the first occasion of these lectures, as we honored George, that I did not survey the landscape but rather examined a few twigs and bushes.

Collected Memories

1

Perpetrator Testimony

Another Look at Adolf Eichmann

Since his capture in Argentina in May 1960 and his subsequent trial and execution in Israel, Adolf Eichmann has remained one of the most enduring symbols of Holocaust evil, though the precise nature of that evil has been hotly contested. To Hannah Arendt the character of Eichmann posed a "dilemma between the unspeakable horror of the deeds and the undeniable ludicrousness of the man who perpetrated them" that could only be solved by understanding him as an exemplar of the "banality of evil."[1] In the latest contribution to this polemic, Yaacov Lozowick has argued that Eichmann cannot be characterized by the commonplace kinds of evil so often encountered, that is indifference, selfishness, or heartlessness in the face of the harm one does to others. Rather Eichmann exemplified willful evil, a man who consciously strove to maximize the harm he did to others.[2] For the record, let me state that I consider Arendt's concept of the "banality of evil" a very important insight for understanding many of the perpetrators of the Holocaust, but not Eichmann himself. Arendt was fooled by

Eichmann's strategy of self-representation in part because there were so many perpetrators of the kind he was pretending to be.

But my task here is not to focus on Eichmann as the symbol of perpetrator evil. It is rather to examine his voluminous postwar testimonies as a source for writing Holocaust history. Historians almost invariably prefer contemporary documents to after-the-fact testimony. However, documents do not speak for themselves and can be interpreted differently. Such is certainly the case in the long running debate over the origins of the Final Solution and, particularly, over Hitler's role in and the timing of the decision-making process. One way historians attempt to resolve disputes about the meaning of documents and the mind-set of their authors is to consult the subsequent testimony of those who were involved in writing them. In this case, of course, the chief authors of Nazi policy—Adolf Hitler, Heinrich Himmler, and Reinhard Heydrich—did not survive to testify. The same holds for many key figures in the lower echelons such as Odilo Globocnik or Christian Wirth, the creators of the Operation Reinhard camps of Belzec, Sobibor, and Treblinka. Rudolf Höss, the commandant of Auschwitz, did survive and testify. However, Auschwitz did not take on its role as a central killing center until the Final Solution was already underway.[3] Moreover, most historians now concur that however vivid and important his memories might be for certain events, Höss's dating and chronology were hopelessly confused. In particular, he telescoped key events in 1941 and 1942, so his testimony cannot resolve disputes over dating during that period.[4]

There was one man who both inhabited a unique vantage point at the very center of the regime (as Reinhard Heydrich's advisor for Jewish affairs) and testified voluminously after the war. This is, of course, Adolf Eichmann. When I have suggested to my colleagues that we must take seriously Eichmann's repeated testimony to the effect that he learned from Heydrich in the fall of 1941 of Hitler's order for the physical destruction of the Jews, I have met with either embarrassed silence or open skepticism.

How can I be so gullible? Don't I know that Eichmann's testimony is a useless conglomeration of faulty memories on the one hand and calculated lies for legal defense and self-justification on the other? From it we can learn nothing of value about what actually happened during the war, only about Eichmann's state of mind after the war. These are documents that reveal how Eichmann wished to be remembered, not what he did.

I have no quarrel with those who insist that we must be very cautious and skeptical about using the Eichmann testimony, but I do not believe that such a potentially valuable source can be dismissed summarily without first examining it closely. Thus I want to examine the Eichmann testimonies in the light of two questions: which parts, if any, can be deemed possibly or even probably accurate and reliable, and what, if anything, do they tell us about the decisions for the Final Solution?

As a starting point, let us establish what constitutes the Eichmann testimonies.[5] Beginning in 1956 Eichmann began a long series of tape-recorded interviews with the Dutch journalist and former SS man Willem Sassen and hand-corrected some of the resulting transcripts. He also wrote another memo on Nazi Jewish policy, referred to as file number 17. About three-quarters of the Sassen transcripts and file number 17 were available at the Eichmann trial, and selected portions were submitted in evidence.[6] For years the tapes were in the possession of a Swiss publisher but have just recently been given to the Bundesarchiv. Irmtrud Wojak, who listened to the tapes and compared them with the transcripts, has ascertained that there are a further seven reels of recorded interviews that were not transcribed. She has also confirmed that the transcripts, if not word perfect, nonetheless accurately reflect Eichmann's statements at the time.[7]

Portions of the Sassen testimony have been published. Sassen sold the rights to *Life* to construct and publish abridged versions of his transcripts, and this version appeared in late 1960.[8] The transcripts were also taken by Eichmann's widow, Vera, and his sons to Rudolf Aschenauer, a German lawyer who specialized in defending those accused of committing Nazi crimes. He edited them for publication by the right-wing Druffel Verlag in 1980 as the posthumous memoirs entitled *Ich, Adolf Eichmann.*[9] Aschenauer interspersed the text with long apologetic sections of his own and also added occasional footnotes alleging to the reader that on occasion Eichmann was himself mistaken, such as when Eichmann referred to a Hitler order for the Final Solution. On another occasion he tells the reader that Eichmann was merely making a "joke" when he referred to little wooden huts as gas chambers.[10] In short, Aschenauer adopted the agenda of the interviewer, Sassen, in trying to twist Eichmann's testimony in service of Holocaust minimization or denial on the one hand and Hitler apologetics on the other.[11] Aschenauer also admitted to stylistic enhancements.

Clearly, Aschenauer exercised even far greater editorial intervention than he admitted to in the book. Various robust and embarrassing comments by Eichmann to Sassen that were submitted in evidence at the trial are not to be found in the book. In particular, Eichmann did not hide his Nazi convictions and his anti-Semitism from Sassen.[12] And Eichmann's accounts in the Sassen interviews of key episodes, such as his descriptions of seeing his first mass shooting at Minsk and his first gassing operation at Chelmno, were not included. Even if it were Vera Eichmann who repressed these materials rather than Aschenauer, clearly the latter had to be aware of their conspicuous absence and was therefore complicitous. Of all the Eichmann testimonies, the Aschenauer version is the most dubious and must be treated with the utmost caution.[13] But sorting out and identifying the omissions, distortions, and falsifications of *Ich, Adolf Eichmann* is not my task here.

Ironically, in a publisher's foreword to the Aschenauer volume, the editors of the Druffel Verlag proclaim that Eichmann's 1950s testimonies, given as a free man rather than in captivity, are the only valid ones. Yet at the trial in Jerusalem, it was the prosecutor Gideon Hausner who wanted the Sassen transcripts admitted into evidence, since they included remarks revealing of Eichmann's own sense of self-importance and his anti-Semitism in contrast to his carefully crafted statements to the contrary in court. Eichmann vigorously opposed their being admitted into evidence. It was mere "pub talk," he claimed, since he had been drinking red wine throughout the interviews.[14] Moreover, Sassen had constantly egged him on to embellish for the sake of journalistic sensationalism and had then falsely transcribed the tapes.[15]

In Jerusalem Eichmann provided no less than five additional testimonies. The first are his pretrial interrogations with Avner Less that began in May 1960 and continued into early 1961. The total record of these interrogations comprises more than thirty-five hundred typescript pages and has now been published in two of the Israeli Ministry of Justice's nine-volume set entitled *The Trial of Adolf Eichmann*.[16] Initially, Less did not confront Eichmann with any documents but let him tell his own story.

At an early point in the interrogations, Less encouraged Eichmann to write up a chronology or life story, which he began to do in late May. This became the second postcapture testimony, the 127-page, handwritten "Meine Memoiren."[17] From August 12 to September 14, 1999, they were published by *Die Welt*, which proclaimed them to be a sensational new discovery, though they had been cited in academic literature since 1985.[18]

In June 1960, one month into the interrogations, when Eichmann had not yet finished writing "Meine Memoiren," Avner Less began confronting him with documents. First in this regard was the testimony of Rudolf Höss, which was highly incriminating. Höss alleged that in the summer of 1941 Eichmann had visited Auschwitz and explained the inadequacies of the firing-squad and gas-van methods of killing. Eichmann had later helped select the sites for Bunkers 1 and 2 in Birkenau and then obtained approval for the use of Zyklon B as the killing gas. The Israeli prosecution tended uncritically to accept the Höss accounts of both chronology and Eichmann's role, even if subsequently many historians,

myself included, do not. For the purpose of evaluating the Eichmann accounts, this point in mid-June 1960 is crucial. Henceforth, all of Eichmann's testimonies must be seen in light of his
strongly felt need to defend himself against the Höss accusations.

When Eichmann began meeting with his defense attorney,
Robert Servatius, he composed handwritten timelines. These were
based on his memory, his reading of the early Holocaust histories
by Poliakov and Reitlinger, and documents he could remember
from the Less interrogations. These handwritten timelines, along
with other notes, were given by Servatius to the Bundesarchiv
Koblenz.[19] They constitute the third version of Eichmann's postcapture testimonies.

Before trial, Eichmann and Servatius were given access to the
more than sixteen hundred documents that the prosecution had
collected. Eichmann then testified in thirty-two court sessions in
Jerusalem between June 20 and July 24, 1961. The record of this
courtroom testimony and cross-examination, Eichmann's fourth
postcapture account, fills more than four hundred fifty printed
pages of another volume of *The Trial of Adolf Eichmann*.[20]

In August 1961, following his courtroom testimony, Eichmann
wrote his second set of handwritten memoirs entitled "Idols" or
"False Gods" (Götzen). This text, in three parts, and of some five
hundred pages as well as hundreds of pages of notes, had been
kept sealed in the Israeli State Archives under the rationale that
the executed Eichmann should not have the last word. They were
finally released in the spring of 2000 in the midst of the Irving-
Lipstadt trial, when the Israelis wanted to avoid any appearance
of suppressing evidence. In this fifth and final postcapture account, Eichmann acted not only as memoirist but also as a historian, citing and quoting documents at length.[21]

The various Eichmann testimonies are truly staggering in their
total volume. But how, if at all, can they be used? Even more than
most memoirs, the Eichmann testimonies, both before and after
capture, are consciously calculated attempts at self-representation,
self-justification, and legal defense. It must be said as emphatically

as possible that, at the core of these testimonies, there are three monstrous falsehoods that are central to his whole enterprise.

First, Eichmann claimed that he was not an anti-Semite! "Personally I have no hatred" against Jews, he explained. His stepmother had Jewish relatives by an earlier marriage, and his parental home was thus free of anti-Semitism. He had played with the children of his father's Jewish friends. He once kissed a pretty half-Jewish cousin on the cheek, and one afternoon in Austria he had even walked down the street and sat at a café with a Jewish acquaintance while wearing his Nazi pin on his lapel. He rejected Julius Streicher and the so-called "Stürmer methods," and he never paid any attention to the anti-Semitic propaganda of the party's publications.[22] When he worked with Jewish functionaries like Dr. Löwenherz in Vienna, he claimed that they were "on the same footing" and worked on a "mutual basis."[23] How, in the light of such behavior, he asked rhetorically, could anyone accuse him of anti-Semitism?

Second, Eichmann portrayed himself in his early career, from the mid-1930s until 1941, as an "idealist" and, indeed, a veritable Zionist. He was "possessed" by the idea of helping the Jews through finding a territory for them. "My sole endeavor was . . . to make some suggestions or other that somewhere . . . land be placed under the feet of the Jews," he told Less. He and the Jewish leadership had worked harmoniously together in a common enterprise of emigration. But they had been thwarted by the petty, small-minded, "dried-up bureaucrats" *(trockner Beamter)* from the Interior Ministry, Finance Ministry, Foreign Office, etc., who had no passion for and no inner connection to their work and obstructed everything he had tried to accomplish.[24] As Irmtrud Wojak has noted, Eichmann consistently tried to reframe his zealous efforts on behalf of "forced emigration" into a *Lebensretter* or "lifesaver" defense.[25]

With the outbreak of the war and the end of emigration, he claimed to have given birth to three great ideas. First, he had thought of creating an autonomous and self-governing state for the Jews in Poland (like Slovakia, not the Protectorate, he claimed), which was ruined by Hans Frank.[26] Second, he had planned for Madagascar as an autonomous and self-governing state, an idea that was then ruined by Foreign Office interference.[27] Finally, he had proposed Theresienstadt and its hinterland as a suitable residence for some ten thousand Czech Jews, but no hinterland was granted, and importuning Gauleiters had insisted on sending German Jews there as well. This led to overcrowding, and his plan for an idyllic Jewish community was transformed into both a propaganda trick to mislead the outside world and a transit camp for deportations to Auschwitz.[28] With the successive failure of his three great ideas, Eichmann complained that his "dream" had been shattered and his "last hope" had disappeared.[29] Henceforth, he was "simply a tool in the hands of stronger powers and stronger forces and of an inexorable fate."[30]

His third great lie was that from that point on he was an utterly passive receiver of orders, who took no initiatives and made no decisions. He simply obeyed. He had nothing to do with killing Jews, though admittedly he played a minor role in their evacuation. But even here he was not the "mainspring" but a minor figure. His superiors made decisions about deporting Jews. Collaborators in occupied countries rounded them up. His subordinates, like Rolf Günther and Franz Novak, scheduled the trains with the Transportation Ministry. And Heydrich's chief rival within the SS, the Economic and Administrative Main Office of Oswald Pohl, ran the death camps in which the deportees were killed.[31]

In addition to these three colossal lies, Eichmann told innumerable little lies when confronted with a succession of incriminating documents and testimony. When faced with "smoking pistol" documents that could not be explained away, he simply claimed they were forgeries.[32] But it is not my task here to expose in detail either these numerous little lies or the falsity of Eichmann's overall self-representation. It is worth noting, however, just how transparent and absurd this misrepresentation is. Eichmann was not a particularly subtle or skilled liar, a point I think worth keeping in mind when evaluating those aspects of his testimony that I do wish to study in detail.

Clearly anyone who wants to dismiss Eichmann's testimonies on the grounds of their demonstrated unreliability and shameless self-serving lies can easily do so, and many of my colleagues have done precisely this. But what if our default position is not to dismiss everything Eichmann said and wrote just because he was lying most of the time, but rather to ask what among this mass of lies might nonetheless be of help to the historian, given his unique vantage point and the sheer volume of his testimony? Christian Gerlach is justifiably cautious but not totally dismissive. He argues that these testimonies "cannot serve as the exclusive, or even the main, basis of any historiographical arguments" and "that even the most thorough interpretation of Eichmann's accounts *alone* (italics mine) cannot achieve a sure evaluation of what really happened." He continues: "All of Eichmann's statements are fundamentally unreliable, and none of them can, *by themselves* (italics mine), provide firm ground for any factual interpretation. The only method that can ensure some certainty is to use the interrogations merely as supportive evidence in tandem with a sufficient mass of contemporary documents, and possible observations by other witnesses."[33]

If one accepts the tenor of Gerlach's careful warning, and I do, how should one go about trying to sift nuggets of useful information from the mass of mendacious sludge? I would suggest the following. First, the self-interest test. When Eichmann made statements against self-interest, or when he was in a situation where telling the truth was in his self-interest, a closer look is merited. Second, the vividness test. When Eichmann described events with an unusual attention to details of visual memory, the actual occurrence of those events should be seriously considered, even if Eichmann's framing of those events, in other words, the meaning of his participation in them, should still be viewed very skeptically.

Third, the possibility test. When Eichmann's claims are not contradicted or proven impossible even in light of the more extensive documentation now available, they should not be summarily rejected. And fourth, the probability test. When Eichmann's accounts coincide with or fit a pattern of events suggested or established by other documentation, they can be viewed not only as possible but also as probable.

I would like to focus on the multiple accounts of eight particular events from 1941 and 1942 that Eichmann related by his own choice, at a time when no other documentation provided any evidence of his presence, much less participation, in them. These multiple accounts were given both before and after he was confronted with the Höss testimony, which became the basis for the prosecution's alternative narrative and chronology that he was contesting. The admission of his role in these eight events in the first place was against self-interest. Once these events had been admitted, however, it became very much in his self-interest in the case of some, though not all, of them to get the chronology right. When preparing his timelines for Servatius in the latter half of 1960, he asked rhetorically: "Why do I lay so much importance on all of this? Because I must prove Höss the archliar, that I had nothing at all to do with him and his gas chambers and his death camp, because I could not at all have been with him at that time."[34]

The eight events are as follows. First, Eichmann admitted that in the fall of 1941 he was summoned to Heydrich, who informed him of the Hitler order for the physical destruction of the European Jews and sent him to Globocnik in Lublin to report on the latter's preparations. Second, the Gestapo chief Heinrich Müller sent him to Minsk to witness a mass shooting. Third, he drove through Lwow (Lemberg), where his local Security Police host showed him a mass grave from which blood was spurting like a "geyser" or "fountain." Fourth, Müller sent him to Chelmno to witness the gas van in action. Fifth, he made two additional trips to Lublin to carry orders, one signed by Heydrich and the other by Müller, to Globocnik. Sixth, he first visited Auschwitz at a time when gassing was done in the two converted farm houses in the woods outside Birkenau. Seventh, he witnessed a gassing at Treblinka. And eighth, he flew to Kiev to make a presentation to Himmler in the presence of Müller.

Let us examine the multiple accounts of these eight events in reverse order. Eichmann described his trip to Kiev to report personally to Himmler three times. In "Meine Memoiren" Eichmann wrote how he flew in a two-engine plane along with a number of high-ranking officers from Breslau to Kiev. He proceeded to Himmler's field headquarters in a former cadet school, where he waited many hours. Müller suddenly appeared and together they were ushered into Himmler. Eichmann delivered a brief five-minute report, based on a single typed page he had stuck in his pocket, on statistics of Jewish emigration. It was his first audience with Himmler, and he dated it to the fall of 1941.[35] On the timeline he shifted the date of this trip to the spring of 1942.[36] In the court testimony he reverted to the fall of 1941 date, tying his report on emigration statistics to Himmler's mid-October 1941 prohibition of further Jewish emigration.[37]

We now know from the Himmler appointment calendar that Müller and Eichmann did have a joint audience with Himmler, but it took place on August 11, 1942, and lasted up to ninety minutes.[38] We can see from the length of time and date that the report was neither brief nor about Jewish emigration. As Himmler had just given the order to complete the Final Solution insofar as possible by the end of the year, presumably Eichmann gave a lengthy report on the number of Jews, country by country, still to be killed. It was precisely such a key role in the Final Solution that Eichmann was denying, and hence his misrepresentation of both the date and meaning of the report to Himmler.

In his interview with Less, Eichmann volunteered that he had been sent to Globocnik by Müller to report on Treblinka. Accompanied by Globocnik's assistant, Hans Höfle, he arrived at the camp when it was in operation. First they saw the train station, with the sign "Treblinka," that looked like a train station anywhere in Germany. Through the wire fence he saw a column of naked Jews entering a large "hall-like" *(Saalähnliche)* building to be gassed.[39] He referred to this Treblinka visit on only one other occasion, when in the courtroom he admitted to having seen the "dummy railway station" at Treblinka. He dated the trip to probably the summer or perhaps the autumn of 1942.[40] Since Treblinka did not begin operating until late July 1942, this dating is quite plausible.

Before he had been confronted with the Höss testimony, Eichmann told Less that he had first visited Auschwitz when he had been sent by Müller to report on the "expansion construction" *(Erweiterungsbauten)*. The camp was still very small, and Höss showed him the "little cottages" *(Häuschen)* in the woods and explained how the gassing was done with Zyklon B in the form of waferlike pellets that looked like beer coasters *(Pappendeckeln, Papptabletten, Biertellern)*.[41] After Less confronted him with the Höss testimony that had Eichmann visiting several times in the summer of 1941 and helping with the subsequent selection of the bunker sites and the type of gas, Eichmann reiterated his story. When he first came to Auschwitz, the killing with Zyklon B in the "initial little cottages" *(kleinen Anfangshaüschen)* was already underway.[42] In his timeline Eichmann dated this first visit to Auschwitz to the spring or early summer of 1942. He had seen the two peasant farms *(Bauernschäfte)* where gassing was done with "coasterlike wafers" *(Pappendeckeln)*, and he also remembered a "special blooming of flowers" *(eine besondere Blumenfälle)*.[43] In "False Gods," Eichmann again dated his first trip to Auschwitz to the "peak of spring" *(Hochfrühjahrzeit)* because of his memory of the "blooming gardens."[44]

We now know that the first major gassings in Bunker 1 in the forest behind Birkenau took place on May 5 and 12, 1942, with the deportation of nine hundred Jews from Dombrowa and fifteen hundred Jews from Sosnowiec. By the end of June over twenty thousand Jews from East Upper Silesia had perished in Bunker 1.[45] During this period Bunker 2 was also being prepared and was operational by the end of June.[46] Höss himself remarked in his autobiography, "During the spring of 1942 hundreds of vigorous men and women walked all unsuspecting to their death in the gas chambers, under the blossom-laden fruit trees of the 'cottage' orchard. This picture of death in the midst of life remains with me to this day."[47] That Eichmann would have been sent to report on the first mass gassings in Bunker 1 is plausible. That Eichmann, like Höss, had a strong visual memory of the spring blossoms on this occasion makes it even probable that he was in Birkenau to witness Höss's first major gassing action amidst the blooming orchards of Bunker 1 in May 1942.

In the *Life* excerpt of 1960, Eichmann admitted that he carried an order from Heydrich to Globocnik "to start liquidating a quarter million Polish Jews."[48] In the Aschenauer memoirs, Eichmann was sent by Heydrich as a courier to deliver personally to Globocnik the order to kill 250,000 Jews. At that time he did not recognize the Lublin camp (here he is presumably referring to Majdanek, which he would have driven past on his first visit to Lublin in the fall of 1941), for it now had a beautiful police quarters, guest house, office buildings, and even drawing rooms where Globocnik showed him models of the future SS "strongpoints" he was going to build in the east. When Eichmann handed over the order, Globocnik put it in his wall safe and proclaimed, "You see, comrade Eichmann, one must always have everything black on white." About one-half year later, Eichmann took a second such order to Globocnik, this time from Müller, for the killing of another 250,000 Jews. This time the camp at the entrance to Lublin, still rather paltry in scale on the previous visit, had now attained a quite respectable size.[49]

In the pretrial interrogation Eichmann attempted to reframe the meaning of his two letters for Globocnik. On two occasions, he admitted, Heydrich had dictated to him a letter for Globocnik to "subject" a further 150,000 or 250,000 Jews to the Final Solution. However, the Jews were allegedly already dead, and these orders were merely retroactive or ex post facto cover for Globocnik. He dated the first of these to some two months after the Wannsee Conference.[50] In "Meine Memoiren," he again admitted to drafting two or three letters from Heydrich to Globocnik, each providing after-the-fact authorization for killing 150,000 or 250,000 Jews.[51] In the timeline Eichmann noted only one trip in the summer of 1942 to carry an ex post facto authorization to Globocnik. He noted the letter must have been signed by either Himmler or Müller, since Heydrich was already dead.[52] In court, after Eichmann had once again claimed that he had had nothing to do with killing, he was confronted with the Sassen transcript version in which he had carried an order to Globocnik to begin killing Jews. He argued that the meaning of the Sassen transcript was wrong and repeated his claim that the order was an after-the-fact authorization, as the Jews were already dead.[53]

Eichmann's postcapture accounts are unpersuasive, and this is the rare case in which the detailed Aschenauer account is the only one that survives close examination. If he took the first letter two months after the Wannsee Conference, as he inadvertently admitted to Less, then this letter had to be in connection with the beginning of Operation Reinhard, which commenced with the clearing of the Lublin ghetto on March 16. Likewise, if the first letter was dictated by Heydrich, it could not have been ex post facto authorization in the summer after Globocnik had killed his first quarter million Jews, for Heydrich was already mortally wounded on May 25. Transparently, after having admitted to the letters, Eichmann was trying to minimize their significance and hence downplay his own importance in line with his defense strategy. As in the case of the audience with Himmler, the episodes of bringing killing orders to Globocnik threatened his defense strategy of belittling his own significance, and Eichmann lied about them. In this case it was not the uncovering of new documentation but the inconsistencies in his own story that unmasked him.

Of all the eight episodes under examination, Eichmann's visit to the death camp of Chelmno is related with the least variation if one makes allowance for the questionable terminology of the *Life* account excerpted from the Sassen transcripts. In this version Eichmann was sent by Müller to report on the gassing operation near Lodz (Litzmannstadt) in the winter of 1941–42.[54] His local hosts explained the use of carbon monoxide from exhaust gas during the drive from Lodz to the camp. Upon arrival, he saw "thousands" of Jews being loaded into "buses" [*sic*] with closed windows. A "doctor" suggested that Eichmann look through a peephole from the driver's seat, but he could not because his "knees were buckling" under him. The "bus" with Eichmann aboard drove for about fifteen minutes to reach its destination, where according to Eichmann, "hell opened up" for him for the first time. The bus backed up to a pit some two meters deep. When the doors of the bus were opened, the corpses were thrown into a pit, where one man pulled gold teeth with a pair of pliers. Eichmann was too shaken to time the operation with a stopwatch, a failure for which Müller chided him on his return.[55]

The Aschenauer version omits any reference to this episode entirely, but Eichmann repeated it at length to Less. It was late 1941 or early 1942. The weather was cold, but there was no snow. At the Chelmno camp, which he misnamed Culm, Eichmann saw Jews undress in a large room. A large closed truck backed up to a ramp, and the naked Jews were forced up the ramp into the truck. When the doors were closed, Eichmann did not accept the doctor's offer to look through the peephole, but he heard the screams. Eichmann followed the truck and then witnessed the most horrible sight he had seen in his life. The truck drove up to a long pit, the corpses were thrown out, and gold teeth were pulled.[56] In "Meine Memoiren" Eichmann basically repeated the same story and added that the experience haunted him in his dreams, and henceforth he had to drink to get to sleep.[57]

Citing Reitlinger that Chelmno began operations at the end of December, Eichmann placed this trip on his timeline to "the beginning of 1942" but before the Wannsee Conference of January 20. In a brief note he also asked himself if the visit might have been in February or March.[58] In court he dated the trip to the "end of December, or shortly thereafter," on one occasion and "in the winter 1941/42" on another.[59] And in "False Gods" he gave the date as January 1942.[60] As Chelmno in fact began operations on December 8, Eichmann could have visited there in either December or January, before the Wannsee Conference. His gruesome description of the gassing operation, down to the details of the ramp, peephole, burial pits, and teeth pulling, is confirmed by other sources. There is no reason to doubt the basic account of what he saw and when, even if the description of his personal reaction is clearly self-serving and calculated.

If Eichmann saw his first gassing action at Chelmno, he witnessed his first mass shooting in Minsk. Again this episode is entirely omitted from the Aschenauer version, but told in detail in the *Life* article. In this version, late in 1941 but before the trip to Chelmno, Müller sent Eichmann to Minsk to report on a shooting of Jews. When he reported to the local SS commander, he was told: "Fine, tomorrow five thousand of them are getting theirs." When Eichmann arrived at the site the following morning, the shooting was already underway, and he could only see the finish. It was very cold, and he was wearing a long leather coat that reached to his ankles. He watched the last group of Jews undress, walk one hundred to two hundred yards to the pit, and jump in, "without offering any resistance whatsoever. Then the men of the squad banged away into the pit with their rifles and machine guns." The scene lingered in Eichmann's memory, he said, because there were children in the pit. One woman held up her child of a year or two, pleading. Eichmann was standing so close that when the child was hit, bits of brains splattered onto his long leather coat, and his chauffeur had to help him clean it off. On the long drive back to Berlin, Eichmann said he hardly spoke a word.[61]

In the Avner Less interrogation, Eichmann altered the account in a number of ways, but in particular, dating it in sequence after the visit to Chelmno. After Müller ordered Eichmann to report on the shooting of Jews in Minsk, he drove through the site of the "double battle" of Bialystok-Minsk, where he remembered seeing the remains of a burnt-out Russian tank. Upon reaching Minsk, he stayed overnight. He got to the killing site late and saw young men with the Totenkopf insignia shooting at the edge of a large pit. He looked into the pit and remembered seeing a woman with her arms held back. His knees gave way, and he climbed into his car and drove to Lwow. After his frightful experience in Minsk, he particularly remembered the "friendly scene" of the train station built in Lwow to celebrate the sixtieth year in the reign of Franz Josef. Upon visiting the Security Police station, he related to his host what he had seen in Minsk and allegedly complained that young men were being turned into sadists. His host immediately confirmed that they were shooting there as well and drove Eichmann past a mass grave, from which spurted a "stream of blood" *(Blutstrahl)* like a geyser.[62]

In "Meine Memoiren" he merely listed Treblinka, Minsk, Lwow, and Auschwitz as places he had visited after Chelmno. He gave no details but described the cumulative effect: "Corpses, corpses, corpses. Shot, gassed, corpses being burned, and fountains of blood pressured up out of the mass graves. An inferno. A hell."[63] In his timeline Eichmann noted the winter coat he was wearing and placed his Minsk trip in the winter of 1942 but after the Wannsee Conference. Now, however, he placed his trip to Lwow, where he saw the "fountain of blood" *(Blutfontane)* in the summer of 1942, in connection with the trip he had made to deliver the letter to Globocnik.[64] In court he recounted again that he was wearing his winter coat in Minsk when he saw the child being shot out of its mother's arms, and again he placed this event after the visit to Chelmno. And again he associated his trip to Lwow, where he "passed a site where Jews had been shot some time before and where—apparently as a result of the pressure of the gasses— the blood was shooting out of the earth like a fountain," with his summer trip to Globocnik.[65] In his final account, Eichmann placed the Minsk trip in January 1942. He made the trip by car, it was bitter cold, he wore a long leather coat, and he took along a large reserve of alcohol. He arrived at the site late, saw the child shot in the hands of its mother, and had to have bits of brains cleaned from his coat. On the drive back to Berlin, he drank schnapps like it was water and thought about his own children.[66]

His trip to Lwow could have taken place on either of the two dates that Eichmann gave. Mass shootings began in eastern Galicia in early October 1941 and continued into December, so he could have been shown any number of mass graves at that time. And as Peter Witte has noted, many witnesses attest to the fact that in the intense summer heat of the summer of 1942, rapid decomposition caused a reddish-black fluid to flow out of many of the mass graves.[67]

Concerning the shooting in Minsk, Eichmann offered conflicting dates of late fall 1941 and early 1942. According to Christian Gerlach, the undoubted expert on the Holocaust in Belarus, only two shootings would fit an Eichmann trip during cold weather: the massacres of November 7–11, 1941, or March 2–3, 1942. Gerlach thinks that there is "scarcely any doubt" that the latter date is correct and that Eichmann was there to arrange for the resumption of deportations.[68] The problem with this dating is that in every account Eichmann spoke of driving to and from Minsk by automobile, and we know from other documents that he was in Berlin on March 4 meeting with his Jewish experts.[69] Moreover, he was simultaneously planning two other meetings that took place in Berlin on March 6.[70] In my opinion it is much more likely that this trip occurred in November, as he suggested in his first account, and preceded his trip to Chelmno.

The massacres of November 7–11, 1941, took place in order to make room in the Minsk ghetto for the imminent arrival of transports from the Reich. Indeed, the first trainload of Jews had already departed from Hamburg on November 8 and arrived on November 11. Eichmann's task at this time was to organize the deportations from Germany and ensure their reception further east. Clearly he had every motive to alter the date of this trip in order to hide his crucial role in ensuring that the local German authorities had massacred Minsk Jews and were ready to receive German Jews.[71]

Before we examine the last of the eight episodes under consideration, it is worthwhile pausing to take stock of what we can conclude up to this point. First, Eichmann's participation in all of these episodes would have remained unknown if Eichmann had not confessed to them. Only in the case of the report to Himmler has evidence come to light through documentation discovered at a much later date. Second, these admissions were contrary to self-interest. He had no motive to invent them, if in fact they had not actually occurred. Third, his description of each of the events has a distinct sense of vividness and authenticity and is compatible with what we know from other sources, even if the dating and context that Eichmann provided were often false. The dates of his visits to Chelmno, Birkenau, and Treblinka seem reasonable. Either of the two dates for witnessing the "blood fountain" near Lwow is possible. In the case of the Minsk shootings and the letters to Globocnik, I think that he moved the dates back. In the case of the report to Himmler, he moved the date forward. In all cases, Eichmann systematically tried to minimize the significance of his role in line with his overall defense strategy, and these cases of false dating were a transparent part of this strategy.

Fourth, once the prosecution confronted Eichmann with the Höss accusation that he had come to Auschwitz and discussed the inadequacies of shooting and the gas vans in the summer of 1941, a new element had to be factored into his defense strategy. Now, ironically, he had a strong motive either to tell the truth or, if he were going to falsify dating, to do so by moving key events to a later point in time. As he ceaselessly reminded first Avner Less and then the court, he could not have talked with Höss in the summer of 1941 about the problems of shootings and gas vans if he had not been to Chelmno and Minsk until the winter or Auschwitz until the spring of 1942. Once having admitted against self-interest to witnessing these events, it was in his self-interest to tell the truth about these particular dates. Moreover, Eichmann seemed to be fully aware of this, as he actually pleaded with Less to provide documents that would permit him to reconstruct his chronology more accurately.[72]

The examination of Eichmann's involvement in the seven episodes we have discussed can tell us a great deal about both his own role in the Final Solution and his postwar defense strategy. But it has not fundamentally affected what we know about the Final Solution. Such is not the case with the last episode, however. Here I will argue that Eichmann's testimony is in fact a significant piece of evidence concerning the state of mind and intentions of the Nazi leaders in the autumn of 1941 that is both compatible with existing documentation and adds to our understanding. Let us examine first the various Eichmann testimonies, with special attention to all of their confusion and inconsistencies, and then the surrounding documentation.

In the *Life* account, Eichmann testified that "in the latter part of 1941" Heydrich sent him to visit a place he named Majdanek, which he characterized as a Polish village near Lublin. There a German police captain showed him "how they had managed to build airtight gas chambers disguised as ordinary Polish farmers' huts, seal them hermetically, then inject the exhaust gas from a Russian U-boat motor."[73] In the Aschenauer account, Heydrich informed Eichmann of both the end of emigration and the "destruction order" at the "turn of the year 1941/42." According to Eichmann, Heydrich's words were: "I come from the Reichsführer; the Führer has now ordered the physical destruction of the Jews." Heydrich informed him furthermore that Globocnik in Lublin was to use antitank ditches for the "mass liquidation of the Jews." Eichmann was to go there and report back on the progress of the operation. From Lublin Eichmann was taken to meet a police captain. "I was not a little astonished, as this man had had little houses built and hermetically sealed and said to me, 'Here Jews are now being gassed.'"[74]

In both precapture accounts, Eichmann's dating is vague.[75] Furthermore, the claims that gassing was already taking place in this first camp, or that it was Majdanek, are contrary to what we know from other sources. The precapture testimonies, in short, are helpful to neither the historian nor Eichmann's credibility.

To Avner Less Eichmann again quoted Heydrich as telling him: "The Führer has ordered the physical destruction of the Jews." And he was sent to report on Globocnik's progress. From Lublin a member of Globocnik's staff, Hans Höfle, drove him to a place he did not know but that had a more Polish sounding name than Treblinka. They halted at a normal wooden house on the right side of the road in a forested area, where they were greeted by a captain of the police. A few other workers were there, and the captain had taken off his coat and seemed to have been help-ing out. They were building two or three little wooden houses perhaps the size of a two- or three-room chalet, in any case not large. The captain then explained the project in a coarse voice and southwest German dialect. He said that everything had been sealed tight, because gas from a Russian U-boat motor would be injected and the Jews would be poisoned. Eichmann then drove back to Berlin and reported to Heydrich and Müller. Eichmann then sought to establish the time of the visit, which he had initially placed in "late summer." Now he corrected himself. He remem-bered that "these wood houses were in . . . a deciduous forest, a rather thick deciduous forest, very large trees, and their leaves were in full color. . . . Thus that was 1941 in autumn."[76]

In later parts of the interrogation, Eichmann added further relevant information. When relating his first sight of the two peas-ant farm houses converted into Bunkers 1 and 2 at Birkenau, he described the "little cottages" in Birkenau as "the same cottages" as "in that forest in Poland" (*dieselben Häus'chen . . . wie in diesem*

Wald in Polen). He also added emphatically that in the first camp outside Lublin the motor was not yet there and the installation had not yet been put into operation. On the suggestion of Less, Eichmann conceded that possibly the place was Belzec, of which he remembered hearing.[77]

In his first handwritten memoirs, at a point still before being confronted with the Höss accusations, Eichmann did not try to date this trip. He related the identical story about hearing of the Führer order from Heydrich and being sent to Lublin to report on Globocnik and his antitank ditches. In this version he added that in Berlin he took his close associate Rolf Günther into his confidence and that driving through Prague he informed the brother Hans Günther as well. After overnighting in Lublin, he was driven by Höfle for about two hours until they reached a wood house on the right side of the road. They met a police captain in shirtsleeves and saw only one other person. The police captain led them over the road and into the forest. He was shown two or three wood houses "still under construction" *(noch im Bau).* The captain explained that they had to be sealed, so that exhaust gas from a Russian U-boat motor could be injected into the rooms. Eichmann was relieved that he did not see any corpses or even any people. He drove back through Prague, where he informed Hans Günther and then went on to Berlin. He reported to Müller and, after getting an appointment through his adjutant, to Heydrich as well.[78]

On the timeline, Eichmann simply dated this trip to Lublin as "fall 1941."[79] In court Eichmann again told how he had learned of the Führer order for the physical destruction of the Jews and then been sent to Lublin to report on Globocnik's use of antitank ditches. He continued: "I saw two medium-sized peasants' cottages, which were being worked on by a captain in the Order Police, whom I found in shirtsleeves. He told me that he had to seal these cottages hermetically and that the Jews were to be gassed here by means of a Russian submarine motor. I did not see any more there—the installation was not yet operating. . . . It cannot yet have been winter, because where these two peasants' cottages were, there was a deciduous forest, and the trees were still in leaf. I would therefore think that it was around the end of summer or autumn, 1941."[80] In a different part of his testimony, Eichmann said that his Lublin trip occurred "a little while before" he went to Lodz to negotiate the reception of the first transports of Reich Jews. He reiterated that the captain was in shirtsleeves and "it must have been the autumn or late autumn, because I can still see the landscape, there were leaves on the trees . . . but there was no killing as yet for a long time—at that time the personnel were just putting up the two small houses."[81]

In "False Gods" Eichmann began the story in the same way. In the fall of 1941 he was summoned to Heydrich who told him: "The Führer has ordered the physical destruction of the Jews. Globocnik has received his relevant instructions from the Reichs-führer. Accordingly Globocnik is supposed to use antitank ditches. I want to know what he is doing and how far he has come." Driven out of Lublin by Höfle for one and one-half or two hours, Eichmann arrived at a small farmer's house in an opening in the forest on the right-hand side of the road. "We were received by an Order Policeman in rolled-up sleeves, who himself apparently had been helping with the physical labor. The style of his boots and the cut of his riding breeches indicated that he was an officer. From the introduction I learned that I was dealing with a captain of the Order Police. In the postwar years his name had long ago escaped me. Only through the literature did I remember again. His name was Wirth." Eichmann was then led along "a small for-est path" on the left side of the road to "two small peasant huts standing under deciduous trees." He did not remember seeing anyone at work there, but Wirth explained that he had to seal all the doors and windows. After the work was concluded, Jews would be killed there with the exhaust gas of a Russian U-boat motor. Eichmann was relieved that he saw no antitank ditches, no Jews, and no corpses. Upon his return, he reported to both Heydrich and Müller.[82] Eichmann stated that this trip took place "shortly before the order to prepare for the first great deportation of Jews" from Germany and his trip to Lodz to extract the agreement of local German authorities to receive these transports.[83]

In all of these accounts Eichmann is perfectly consistent on several important points. The trip occurred in the fall of 1941 on the order of Heydrich, who had informed him of Hitler's order for the physical destruction of the Jews and sent him to report on Globocnik's use of antitank ditches. In all of these accounts he was driven by an assistant of Globocnik, usually identified as Höfle, some distance from Lublin. He was not shown the expected antitank ditches. Instead, a police captain in shirtsleeves took him from a lone wood house on the right-hand side of the road into the forest on the left-hand side and showed him his preparations for killing Jews with carbon monoxide exhaust gas in sealed rooms. In the two final accounts Eichmann explicitly placed this trip to Lublin before his trip to Lodz, where he went to arrange for the reception of Jewish transports from the Reich. The major inconsistency is in the differing descriptions, even within the same accounts, of the wooden houses that he saw in the forest. On two occasions Eichmann spoke of them as if they were new buildings "under construction." On three occasions he refers to them as peasant huts (like those in Birkenau) that Wirth was sealing up in order to convert them into gas chambers. This, in fact, is not a minor point, as we shall see.

Historians who do not accept Eichmann's dating of this trip to the fall of 1941 have pursued three major lines of attack on the credibility of his account. First, they argue that Eichmann falsified the date as a part of his defense strategy of hiding behind a binding Hitler order. Second, Poles who were drafted for construction work at Belzec testified that they began work on the first three buildings on November 1, 1941. Third, according to the testimony of Josef Oberhauser, Christian Wirth's adjutant, Wirth did not arrive at Belzec until December 1941. The conclusion these critics draw is that Eichmann did not go to Belzec until the winter of 1941–42. Thus, they argue that one cannot cite Eichmann's testimony about his trip to Lublin in support of dating a Hitler order for the physical destruction of the Jews to the fall of 1941.[84]

In my opinion none of these arguments are convincing. Eichmann's confession concerning his trip to Lublin was against interest, and indeed the prosecution immediately brought to the attention of the court the fact that Eichmann had admitted that he was aware of the ultimate fate of all the Jews he helped to deport in the fall of 1941, even though they were not killed immediately. The standard defense strategy of virtually every other accused Nazi war criminal in the same situation was systematically to deny knowledge of the fate of the deportees until the prosecution could produce incontrovertible evidence concerning their state of mind and awareness on that point, which for Eichmann would have been the Wannsee Conference protocol. Certainly, if Eichmann had not been aware of the intention of the regime to murder the Reich Jews deported in the fall of 1941, he had no motive to make a false confession to incriminate himself in that regard. He did not need to misdate to an earlier point in time and to his own disadvantage his learning of the Hitler order in order to use the defense of superior orders.

Second, the Oberhauser testimony is evidence only that Wirth took command of Belzec in December 1941. It does not preclude that Wirth was also in the Lublin district in the fall of 1941 before the construction of Belzec and Oberhauser's arrival. Indeed one of Wirth's associates testified after the war: "I knew police captain Wirth, the administrative head of various euthanasia institutes, who told me in the late summer of 1941 that he . . . was being transferred to a euthanasia institute in the Lublin area."[85]

Finally, by the end of December, the Polish workers had constructed three large barracks (50 by 12.5 meters, 25 by 12.5 meters, and 12 by 8 meters according to Stanislaw Kozak), not two little wooden huts, while simultaneously seventy Russian prisoners of war in black uniforms had dug the first large grave (50 meters long, 20 meters wide, and 6 meters deep), connected to the future gas chamber by a narrow rail line. They had also encircled the camp with a thick, barbed-wire fence. In short, in any winter visit Eichmann would have encountered a nearly complete camp filled with workers—a scene not remotely similar to anything he described in his testimonies beyond his mention of seeing two (and in one account possibly three) wooden houses under construction.

If the scenario of a winter or spring[86] trip to the forest site beyond Lublin is both contradicted by Eichmann's own description and difficult to reconcile with any rational defense strategy on Eichmann's part, is there an alternative scenario that can be reconciled with the accepted November 1 starting date for the construction of Belzec? I believe so, but the necessary starting point is my admittedly speculative hypothesis that the site Eichmann visited was not the Belzec camp under construction. That site lay alongside the main road and rail line, in sight of the train station and town, which hardly fits Eichmann's description of two small wooden houses or peasant huts at the end of a footpath in the middle of a dense deciduous forest.[87] I would suggest that in September 1941 Wirth had been sent to the Lublin district to experiment with creating a gassing facility on a larger scale than the euthanasia institutes in Germany. He first contemplated converting peasant huts into gas chambers by sealing them hermetically (as Höss was to do with Bunkers 1 and 2 in Birkenau), and this is the site Eichmann was sent to visit in order to inform Heydrich of the latest developments. As Bogdan Musial has recently discovered, the commander of the Gendarmerie in the Lublin district, Ferdinand Herzog, also testified to the existence of "a primitive installation, consisting of a hermetically sealed shack hidden deep in the forest across from Galicia near Belzec" in which gassing was tested.[88]

How does such a scenario fit with the existing state of documentation? We know that in August 1941 Hitler had rejected various proposals to begin deporting Jews to the east, stating that this would not occur "during the war" but only "after the end of the campaign."[89] In the first half of September, Eichmann certainly exhibited no awareness of any imminent change. Based on a "recent consultation" with Eichmann, his SS associate Rolf-Heinz Höppner complained on September 2 that he was hampered in his work "because I do not know the intentions of the Führer" and because no "basic decisions" had been made. The frustrated Höppner felt it was "essential . . . that total clarity prevails about what finally shall happen to those undesirable ethnic elements deported from the greater German resettlement area. Is it the goal to ensure them a certain level of life in the long run, or shall they be totally eradicated."[90] If Eichmann had been unable to help Höppner answer this question, he was equally unhelpful regarding the request of Germans in Serbia eager to deport their Jews. Eichmann rejected this request on September 13, 1941, noting that "residence in Russia and the GG impossible. Not even the Jews from Germany can be lodged there."[91]

Just days later the situation was suddenly transformed. On September 16 and 17, a number of meetings were held involving Hitler, Himmler, Joachim von Ribbentrop, and others. Out of this cluster of meetings, Hitler reached the basic decision to proceed with the deportation of Reich Jews that in August he had deferred until after the war.[92] On September 18, Himmler informed the Gauleiter of the Warthegau, Arthur Greiser, that Hitler wished to empty the Reich of Jews. Thus "as a first step" sixty thousand Jews were about to be deported to the Lodz ghetto, but Greiser was reassured that these Jews would be sent "yet further to the east next spring."[93]

This turning point coincided with the renewed German offensive in the east. On September 12 German troops in the Ukraine had broken through Soviet lines, and by September 16 the encirclement of Kiev was complete. Thus when Hitler met with Himmler, Heydrich, Goebbels, and others in a series of meetings between September 21 and 24, 1941, his mood was optimistic. Hitler assured Goebbels that "the spell is broken. In the next three to four weeks we must once again expect great victories." Hitler believed that by October 15, the serious fighting would be over and Moscow would be encircled. Goebbels also learned from Heydrich that the deportation of the Jews of Berlin "could occur as soon as we arrive at a clarification of the military situation in the east."[94] Following these meetings and having been assured of his appointment as the new Reich Protector of Bohemia and Moravia, Reinhard Heydrich returned to Berlin late on September 24 and then departed for Prague on the afternoon of September 27.[95]

Meanwhile, sometime in September Philipp Bouhler and Viktor Brack of the recently suspended adult euthanasia program visited Odilo Globocnik in Lublin.[96] Among the deactivated euthanasia staff in Berlin, the rumor spread that "something similar" to the euthanasia program was starting in Lublin, only this time it was to be for the Jews.[97] Already between late August and mid-September gassing tests with Zyklon B had been undertaken in Auschwitz.[98] And in mid-September the chemist of Heydrich's crime lab in Berlin, Albert Widmann, traveled to Belarus and undertook test killings with carbon monoxide from automobile exhaust.[99] In short, on the basis of what we know from other documentation, it would not have been unusual if, following the Bouhler-Brack visit to Globocnik, Christian Wirth had also been sent to Lublin to conduct his own experiments. And Eichmann could have been summoned to Heydrich in Berlin on September 17 and 18 or between 25 and 27 preceding the latter's departure for Prague.[100] Eichmann could have reported back to Heydrich either in Prague, which he mentioned traveling through in one account, or in Berlin. (After his afternoon of September 27 departure for Prague, Heydrich visited Berlin again on October 4.)[101]

Eichmann's visit to Lodz, which he said followed his trip to Lublin, can be dated to late September, for on September 29 Eichmann was back in Berlin reporting an alleged agreement of the Lodz authorities to accept twenty thousand Jews and five thousand "Gypsies." On October 7 Regierungspräsident Friedrich Uebelhoer visited Berlin to investigate what Eichmann had reported, and on October 9 he wrote a scathing letter to Himmler, in which he accused Eichmann of "ugly Gypsy-like horse-trading manners" and making false claims about Lodz's reception capacity.[102] On this same day, October 9, that Uebelhoer wrote his complaining letter, Goebbels noted in his diaries that in Berlin the leaves had already turned brown and were falling.[103] Heydrich and Eichmann were together in Prague at a meeting on October 10. Heydrich announced that the deportation of the Reich Jews was to begin on October 15 (the very day Hitler had given earlier for the end of serious fighting in the east), "because the Führer wishes that by the end of this year as many Jews as possible are removed from the German sphere." Eichmann, Heydrich observed, had arranged for the reception of fifty thousand Reich Jews in Lodz, Riga, and Minsk.[104]

Meanwhile in the Lublin district, on October 1 Globocnik wrote to Himmler that he and Higher SS and Police Leader Friedrich Wilhelm Krüger urgently needed a meeting with the Reichsführer-SS in order to present "prepared documentation" concerning, among other matters, the "removal" of alien populations from the General Government. Globocnik and Krüger met with Himmler for two hours on October 13, and on the following day Himmler lunched with Hitler and then had a five-hour meeting with Heydrich that evening.[105]

The repercussions of the Himmler-Globocnik-Krüger meeting on October 13 were immediate, both in Lublin and in Berlin. On that very day Hans Frank had approached the head of the Ostministerium, Alfred Rosenberg, about "the possibility of deporting the Jewish population of the General Government into the occupied eastern territories." However, "for the moment" Rosenberg saw "no possibility for the carrying out of such resettlement plans."[106] Just four days later, Globocnik and Frank met in

Lublin.[107] On that same day local officials there were informed that "the Jews—with the exception of indispensable artisans and the like—will be evacuated from Lublin. To begin with, one thousand Jews will be sent over the Bug River. The SS and Polizeiführer [Globocnik] will be in charge of the implementation."[108] Another four days later, on October 21, Frank justified his prohibition against further ghetto building in his realm, "because the hope exists, in the near future, that the Jews can be deported out of the General Government."[109] In short, in the days immediately following October 13, the same day when Rosenberg refused to accept deportations from the General Government and Himmler met with Globocnik and Krüger, Frank learned that deportations from the General Government would proceed in the near future anyway. The expressed destination was "over the Bug," but what did this mean? On November 1, Polish workers began construction of the death camp alongside the rail line just beyond the train station in Belzec. I would suggest that Wirth's experimental huts deep in the forest had been transformed into plans for a full-fledged death camp capable of receiving continual train transports. Work could not have begun on November 1, if prior planning and supply of materials had not begun immediately following the October 13 meeting at the latest.

Belzec was not, however, an isolated case arising solely from local circumstances and initiatives. A fundamental and fateful change in the policy regarding Jewish emigration occurred in Berlin at exactly the same time. On October 13, Undersecretary Martin Luther of the Foreign Office wrote to Heydrich concerning an approach from the Spanish government. A number of Spanish Jews in Paris had been among the mass of Jews arrested and interned in France following an attack on German military personnel in August. This led the Spanish government to suggest the possibility of evacuating all Spanish Jews, some two thousand, from France to Spanish Morocco if the arrested Spanish Jews would be released. Luther viewed this proposal very favorably, in

line with the basic goal of Nazi Jewish policy to this point of ex-
pelling the Jews from Europe. On October 17, however, just three
days after Himmler's five-hour meeting with Heydrich, Luther received a phone call from the Reich Security Main Office, or
RSHA, opposing the evacuation of Spanish Jews to Morocco.
The RSHA now perceived no solution in such a proposal because
these Jews would be "all too much out of the direct reach of the
measures for a basic solution to the Jewish question to be enacted
after the war."[110] One day later, on October 18, the new policy
was extended from the Spanish Jews to all cases, as Himmler
noted after a telephone conversation with Heydrich: "No emigration by Jews overseas."[111]

In short, the decisions to construct Belzec and end Jewish
emigration coincided exactly with the Himmler-Globocnik and
Himmler-Heydrich meetings of October 13 and 14. But the documents indicate even more widespread results as well. In mid-
October Eichmann's associate Friedrich Suhr accompanied the
Foreign Office Jewish expert, Franz Rademacher, to Belgrade to
deal with the Jewish question in Serbia. After the fate of the adult
male Jews had been settled in a meeting on October 20 (they were
to be killed by the army in mass reprisal shootings), Rademacher
reported on the women, children, and elderly: "Then as soon as
the technical possibility exists within the framework of a total solution to the Jewish question, the Jews will be deported by water-
way to the reception camps in the east."[112] From whom, if not
Eichmann's associate Suhr, could Rademacher have learned
about reception camps for Jewish women, children, and elderly in
the east?

And what was the purpose of such camps? When Rademacher
returned to Berlin five days later, he found waiting a letter of October 23 from an old friend, Paul Wurm, foreign editor of *Der
Stürmer*. Wurm had been visiting Berlin and had just missed seeing
Rademacher, but he had had another interesting conversation of
which he hurried to inform Rademacher in a personal note:

"Dear Party Comrade Rademacher! On my return trip from Berlin I met an old party comrade, who works in the east on the settlement of the Jewish question. In the near future many of the Jewish vermin will be exterminated through special measures."[113] What an extraordinary coincidence that on that very day of October 23, when Wurm encountered visitors from the east to Berlin talking of exterminating Jews through special measures, Eichmann had met in Berlin with his deportation experts, including those from the east, to discuss the impending deportation of fifty thousand Reich Jews to Riga and Minsk that would follow the first wave of deportation to Lodz.[114]

Indeed, what were the plans for the Reich Jews deported to Lodz, Riga, and Minsk? At some point in the fall of 1941, according to the chauffeur of euthanasia killer Herbert Lange, he drove his chief around the Warthegau looking for a suitable site for a camp. He then drove Lange to Berlin for consultations and returned to a village northwest of Lodz in late October or early November, where a team of SS men and Order Police was assembled from both Lodz and Poznan and a work force of Poles began renovating and fencing an old villa in the center of town. The village was Chelmno.[115]

On October 23–25, 1941, Himmler was in Mogilev beyond Minsk. According to the research of Christian Gerlach, Himmler declared that solutions other than shooting would soon be available to kill Jews and specifically spoke of gas chambers. By mid-November the Topf Company had been commissioned to construct a huge crematorium there, and in December the first four-chamber crematorium oven was delivered.[116]

On October 23, while Himmler was beginning his visit in Mogilev, Eberhard Wetzel of the Ostministerium was invited to meet with Viktor Brack, who supervised the euthanasia program out of the Führer Chancellery. According to Wetzel, Brack declared himself ready to aid in the construction of "gassing apparatuses" (*Vergasungsapparate*) on the spot in Riga because they were not in sufficient supply in the Reich. At this time, it might be noted, the prototype of the gas van had been constructed in the motor pool garage of the RSHA but not yet tested on Soviet prisoners of war in Sachsenhausen. Wetzel then sought out Eichmann. Following these two encounters, Wetzel composed a letter for his boss, Rosenberg, to the officials in the Ostland. This draft noted that Reich Jews were going to be sent to Riga. Those capable of labor would be sent "to the east" later, but under the circumstances there would be no objections "if those Jews who are not fit for work are removed with Brack's device."[117]

The climax to this flurry of genocidal anticipation came on the evening of October 25, when Hitler met with Heydrich and Himmler following the latter's return from Mogilev. Hitler recalled his Reichstag prophecy and blamed the Jews for the German lives lost in both wars. "It is good when the terror proceeds us that we are exterminating the Jews. . . . We are writing history anew, from the racial standpoint."[118]

In conclusion, I would note that the Eichmann account about how he learned from Heydrich in the fall of 1941 of the Hitler order for the physical destruction of the Jews as well as his subsequent trip to Lublin to see the very earliest stages of Globocnik's preparations for gassing during the height of autumn colors has been given short shrift in most historical works on the origins of the Final Solution. It is, of course, inconvenient to the current trend in scholarship that emphasizes local and regional initiatives, downplays the role of Hitler, and rejects the notion of clear decision making at the center. It is likewise inconvenient to those who argue that the fundamental change in Nazi policy from a vision of expulsion to a vision of systematic mass murder was not coupled with Hitler's decision to begin deporting Jews from the Third Reich and renewed expectations of an early victory in the east but rather followed much later and in a much more piecemeal fashion.

While the Eichmann account has been dismissed, I would argue that it has not been disproven. Indeed, I would go even further. If historians cannot find "smoking pistol" documents, they must look for pattern and fit among the evidence that is available, even highly problematic evidence like the Eichmann testimonies. When we place both Eichmann's account and his other activities that we know about from surviving documentation into the wider historical reconstruction, the account is not only possible but also, I would argue, quite probable. In turn it helps to illuminate not only the timing of the decisions for the Final Solution but also the intent and vision of the Nazi leadership in the fall of 1941.

2

Survivor Testimonies from Starachowice

Writing the History of a Factory Slave Labor Camp

There are many ways to approach the topic of survivor testimony. Some scholars are primarily interested in the mode of "retelling" and narrative construction. These scholars seek insight from the ways survivors live with their Holocaust memories and how they "talk about those experiences." The focus here is less on content than form, less on the number of survivors interviewed and more on the number of times a survivor has been interviewed.[1] Some have studied survivor testimonies as a source for understanding the nature of identity and identity formation.[2] Others see such testimonies as an attempt both to overcome the "extreme loneliness" of the survivor through reconnecting with society and to thwart the Nazi attempt at the total oblivion of its victims.[3] Yet another approach focuses on survivors' testimonies as a means of studying their trauma and unhealed wounds. The survivors become ex post facto subjects for the study of the enduring effects of suffering and victimization in extremis, even down to the second and third generations.[4] The survivors' stories are also studied as models of resilience and triumph "against all odds."[5] In contrast, other scholars (and here I would mention the important and unsettling work of Lawrence Langer in particular) examine survivor testimonies to affirm the "meaninglessness" of the event. Here the focus is on the cataclysmic rupture that was suffered, and the incapacity of survivors at that time or listeners now to comprehend these experiences through the concepts and vocabulary bequeathed us by the non-Holocaust world. This approach resists our understandable desire to transform these narratives into tales of redemption and triumph of the human spirit.[6] All these approaches emphasize the effects of the Holocaust upon the survivors and how they have remembered and narrated, struggled and coped with those effects rather than the events of the Holocaust itself. The "authenticity" of the survivor accounts is more important than their "factual accuracy." Indeed, to intrude upon the survivors' testimonies with such a banal or mundane concern seems irrelevant and even insensitive and disrespectful.

In another set of approaches to survivor testimony, the focus shifts from the individual to society at large. Underlying one such approach is the study of the emergence of "Holocaust consciousness" and the construction of the concept of the "Holocaust survivor" as distinct from the undifferentiated mass of camp victims and displaced persons confronting the Allied liberators at the end of the war. In the process, the "survivor," initially ignored and then discovered, has been transformed into the "messenger" from another world who alone can communicate the incommunicable. Here again what has been sought is the essence of an ineffable experience, not the narrative recovery of mere events.[7]

Closely related to this approach is the wider issue of the interplay and tension between history and memory, past and present, that has been at the center of much historical discussion in recent years, with ever increasing emphasis on "collective memory." Here the key question is: How is a society's identity and self-understanding both created by and reflected in the selection from and manipulation of survivor accounts to create society's present "collective memory" of the past? As important and interesting as these approaches may be, they are not the approaches to the issue of history, memory, and survivor testimony that I am taking.

Instead, I am looking at memory not in the collective singular but rather in the individual plural, not collective memory but rather collected memories. How may a historian of the Holocaust use a variety of different, often conflicting and contradictory, in some cases clearly mistaken, memories and testimonies of individual survivors as evidence to construct a history that otherwise, for lack of evidence, would not exist?

I first encountered the general problem not with the memories and testimonies of survivors but rather with the postwar interrogations of German perpetrators. Because the Final Solution was a bureaucratic-administrative process and so many of the perpetrators, as a matter of normal procedure, documented their actions at the time, most of what we call "perpetrator history" is based on contemporary German documentation. But in researching the massacres and ghetto-clearing roundups carried out by obscure units such as Reserve Police Battalion 101, the historian has no alternative but to use postwar German testimony. Here the normal problems of forgetfulness as well as unconscious distortion and reinvention of one's past are aggravated by a strong motivation intentionally to lie, mislead, minimize, obfuscate, and feign amnesia. Serious methodological differences over how to deal with such problematic evidence was one source of the radically different interpretations and conclusions reached by Daniel Goldhagen and myself from the same body of interrogations.

The use of survivor testimonies as historical evidence has been even more contested. Most extreme and least serious is, of course, the stance taken by Holocaust deniers, who reject virtually all eyewitness testimony. They routinely dismiss postwar perpetrator testimony as a product of torture and coercion, though in fact the vast bulk of such testimony was the product of investigations by German judicial authorities beginning in the late 1950s, not of allegedly vengeful allies conspiratorially constructing a false victors' history in the immediate aftermath of World War II. Survivors' testimony in turn is dismissed by the deniers as either the hysterical incorporation into memory of false allied propaganda claims or outright lies calculated to defame Germany and defraud it of reparations money. Such blanket dismissal of all postwar testimony by both perpetrator and survivor (except the blatant lies of those facing trial, which are uncritically accepted at face value) is necessitated, of course, by the desperate need to discredit and invalidate this vast body of evidence that renders the deniers' claims totally absurd.

Paradoxically, perhaps the most serious challenge in the use of survivor testimony as historical evidence is posed not by those who are inherently hostile to it but by those who embrace it too uncritically and emotionally. Please allow me two anecdotes to illustrate what I mean. At a conference at the University of Haifa in 1986, Raul Hilberg delivered a paper on the nature of sources for writing Holocaust history. In the course of the discussion, he remarked that in establishing the factual record concerning Nazi policies and measures of persecution, he found contemporary German documents far more reliable than postwar survivor memories. This remark was reported to an Israeli newspaper that exploded in righteous indignation that Hilberg trusted the word of Nazi perpetrators over that of Jewish survivors. An appropriate professional judgment about the varying reliability of different kinds of sources for conveying certain kinds of information was transformed into an inappropriate allegation that such a choice constituted a pernicious moral judgment, that Hilberg deemed Nazis more "trustworthy" than survivors.

Shortly after my book *Ordinary Men* was published, I visited Jerusalem to conduct research at Yad Vashem. On short notice an informal gathering of historians from Yad Vashem and the Hebrew University of Jerusalem was organized to discuss the book. I was among friends, and the atmosphere was collegial. One polite line of criticism (that would be repeated elsewhere in a more strident and accusatory form) was that I had based my study overwhelmingly on the postwar testimonies of perpetrators but had neglected that of survivors, and thus my narrative and conclusions were skewed.

I noted that I had used survivor testimony to establish the chronology of the battalion's murderous rampage in the fall of 1942. For the perpetrators, after the trauma of initiation, one town, one day, and one massacre blurred indistinctly into the next. For the survivors, the particular day in which this itinerant killing squad reached their town and murdered their families was anything but indistinct. They, rather than the perpetrators, were in the best position to give reliable testimony in that regard.

But on several other key questions that was not the case. I wanted to know in particular about the different attitudes and spectrum of behavior within the battalion. And I wanted to know about the transformation of the men over time, how they were changed by what they did. Survivors whose encounter with the battalion was brief, traumatic, and anonymous were simply not in a position to know and remember in this regard.

I then raised a hypothetical example. If I wanted to research the internal dynamics of a unit of Israeli reservists on the West Bank during the Intifada, to learn who and how many shot eagerly and who and how many refused even to fire their guns on Palestinian demonstrators, and to learn how the behavior and attitude of the reservists changed over time, I could scarcely find answers to those questions by interviewing the stone-throwing Palestinians whom they were shooting at in a single town on a single day. The primary source for the internal dynamics of an Israeli reserve unit would have to be the Israeli reservists themselves, no matter how problematic much of their testimony might be.

To my relief, my colleagues did not try to confuse the issue at hand by suggesting that I was somehow comparing Nazi mass killers with Israeli reservists. On the contrary, they saw the point clearly, namely, that a historian must make critical judgments about the use of sources depending upon the questions that are being asked and the varying capacity of the available sources (including eyewitnesses "who were there") to provide reliable information relevant to those questions.

The pitfalls concerning the use of survivor testimony when the emotional desire to believe has been allowed to eclipse the normal critical approach that should apply to any source has, of course, been demonstrated in two public debacles.[8] The early lionization of the Wilkomerski pseudomemoirs only slowly gave way to skeptical investigation and the embarrassing revelation that the author was not in fact a Holocaust survivor. And the conviction of John Demjanjuk in an Israeli court as "Ivan the Terrible" of Treblinka, on the basis of the testimony of Treblinka survivors, had to be overturned by the Israeli Supreme Court when documentation from Soviet archives indicated that he was instead "Ivan the Less Terrible" of Sobibor. I have no doubt that the Treblinka survivors sincerely believed in the truth of their own testimonies. I suspect that even Wilkomerski was sincere though highly disturbed. But the historian needs accuracy, not just sincerity.

More recently, in his book *Neighbors,* Jan Gross has argued for a default position in favor of survivor testimony. "When considering survivors' testimonies, we would be well advised to change the starting premise," he writes. "By accepting what we read in a particular account as fact until we find persuasive arguments to the contrary, we would avoid more mistakes than we are likely to commit by adopting the opposite approach, which calls for cautious skepticism toward any testimony until an independent confirmation of its content has been found."[9] In a situation in which the logical corollary of a German policy of total extermination was to have no survivor witnesses whatsoever, and when in so many cases, there is only a handful of survivors, this is a tempting proposition.[10] But however tempting, this default position still strikes me as too low an evidentiary threshold.

From studying large numbers of survivor testimonies, we do know that there are certain tendencies and recurring patterns. I think that uncorroborated survivor testimony must always be seen in this light as a possible corrective. For instance, Gross argues that "there were no reasons whatsoever for Jews, in their recollection of Shoah episodes they experienced and witnessed, to attribute to Poles those crimes that were in reality perpetrated by the Germans."[11] This is seemingly logical, but from my experience it is empirically incorrect. On the contrary, survivors tend to remember—with greater vividness, specificity, and outrage—the shattering and gratuitous acts of betrayal by their neighbors more than the systematic acts of anonymous Germans. If recognition of such a tendency is combined with the unequivocal documentation that it was explicit German policy at that time to incite local pogroms without leaving any trace of German involvement, the evidence that Gross has worked through would probably render a somewhat less emphatic and more cautious conclusion concerning the relatively minimal German role at Jedwabne that he portrays. While Gross has found much corroboration of the survivor accounts in the testimony of both bystanders and perpetrators for the decisive Polish role in carrying out the massacre of Jedwabne's Jews, I suspect that the German role was not just one of granting permission for the massacre but rather one of active instigation, orchestration, and participation.

The use of survivor testimony, therefore, is not a Holocaust historian's "silver bullet" that will answer all his questions and solve all his problems. Claiming that survivor testimony must be accorded a privileged position not subject to the same critical analysis and rules of evidence as other sources or, even worse, lodging the indiscriminate accusation that a historian has not used survivor testimony as a weapon to discredit both his or her work and character, will not serve the cause of integrating survivor testimony into the writing of Holocaust history. They will merely discredit and undermine the reputation and integrity of Holocaust scholarship itself.

So far I have dealt with negatives, that is, claims both against and for the use of survivor testimony as historical evidence that I consider either unjustified or in need of qualification. Let us now turn to the positive, that is, at least one important way in which I think survivor testimony can be used as historical evidence and what it can tell us. In this regard, I would like to discuss my current research project, a case study of the complex of Jewish factory slave labor camps in Starachowice, a small industrial town in the Radom district in central Poland. This is a camp complex rarely mentioned in surviving German documentation, and only a handful of Germans stationed there during the war were later interrogated. From these scant sources, no adequate history of these camps could be written. But I have located the testimonies of some 173 survivors of the Starachowice camps, and in my opinion they have proven to be an extraordinary source that makes the writing of a history of these camps quite feasible.

Let us look at the nature of these testimonies. The first and smallest group of testimonies was dictated in Poland in the immediate postwar period, the earliest in the summer of 1945. They were kept in such places as the Jewish Historical Institute in Warsaw or the Wiener Library in London, from which copies were sent to Yad Vashem. One very early testimony of a Starachowice survivor is also found in David Boder's pioneering collection of audiotaped testimonies. The second and largest group of testimonies, 116, were collected all over the world by German judicial investigators in the 1960s and are now found in the Central Agency for the Investigation of Nazi Crimes in Ludwigsburg. A third group of testimonies was given in the last three decades. A few were dictated by survivors in Israel for Yad Vashem. But the vast bulk of these late testimonies were recorded in the United States.

The earliest were recorded only on audiotape and donated to the Museum of Jewish Heritage in New York. Most were recorded on videotape and are now found in either the Fortunoff Archive at Yale University, the United States Holocaust Memorial Museum, the Holocaust Survivor Oral History Archive of the University of Michigan–Dearborn, or the Survivors of the Shoah Visual History Foundation in Los Angeles. And finally, one Starachowice survivor has published a book-length memoir.

Almost all of these testimonies, from whatever era, therefore, are oral rather than written communications. But they differ according to the format in which the oral testimonies were taken. The German judicial investigators, needless to say, were trying to find witnesses who could testify in court against suspected Nazi criminals. The investigators thus first took general testimonies, that is, they allowed the survivors to tell their stories, and then they asked a series of focused questions concerning aspects of the testimony of those whom they considered potential witnesses. They had no interest in pursuing questions potentially important to future historians but irrelevant to the case at hand.

In most of the early dictated testimonies of the immediate postwar period and in the initial recorded testimonies of the 1980s, the interviewer was passive. He or she did not visibly intrude with questions or structure the interview. In the more recent 1990s videotaped testimony of the Visual History Foundation, in contrast, the interviewer is more active. The testimony is structured to include prewar, war, and postwar experiences in chronological order, and the interviewer regularly poses a set of questions common to all interviews. One advantage is that survivors are pressed to remember and comment on topics they would otherwise have omitted and to expand on important stories they would otherwise have rushed through. There is one taped interview, for instance, in which the survivor, after talking at length about his harrowing experiences in and escape from the Warsaw ghetto, momentarily could recall little about his nearly two years at Starachowice.

Somewhat flustered, he was about to move on to Auschwitz. However, questions from the interviewer triggered further memories, and he spoke many minutes longer about Starachowice. There are at least several obvious disadvantages, however. For those interested in the psychology and structure of survivor memory and narrative, for instance, the interviews are not pristine. And for the historian, some of the interviewers' questions are frustratingly naïve and uninformed. I remember one kindly and well-intentioned interviewer who obviously knew nothing of the kapo system asking, dumbfounded, "Do you mean it was a fellow prisoner who beat you?" Thereafter, the survivor was obviously reluctant to touch upon difficult and sensitive issues that his naïve interviewer would not understand.

Though only 25 percent of the Jewish prisoners in Starachowice were women, and the last major selection in Starachowice struck the older female prisoners disproportionately hard, nonetheless some 45 percent of these survivor testimonies are by women. As the number of women's testimonies, even in the 1960s, is similarly disproportionate, this cannot be accounted for simply by the longer life spans of female survivors after liberation. It would suggest that the survival rate of women prisoners after Starachowice was higher or a much higher percentage of women survivors have been willing to give postwar testimony than men. Though I do not know the reason for the relatively high number of women's testimonies, it is a pattern that other researchers in collected testimonies have also encountered.[12]

Not surprisingly, the testimonies frequently contradict one another concerning chronology, dates, persons, and events. Indeed, 173 witnesses cannot be expected to have seen, experienced, and remembered the same events in the same way even in far less traumatic circumstances than a Nazi slave labor camp. But if the 173 testimonies make clear the contradictions among survivor accounts, they also reveal a firm core of shared memory. Given that most of the testimonies clustered in three periods—immediate postwar, the 1960s, and the 1980s and 1990s—and that the survivors clustered geographically in three places—Israel, the Toronto area of Canada, and the Boston–New York region of the northeastern United States—I had expected to find patterns of changing and diverging memory. I had expected that as time passed the survivors would speak less and less about sensitive topics like the role of the Jewish camp council and camp police and the resulting tensions within the prisoner community and that they would increasingly cast their narratives in the less ambiguous terms of generic perpetrators and generic victims. I had also expected that as the survivors periodically met with one another regionally and retold their stories to one another, three geographically separate "memory communities" would take shape, increasingly homogeneous within but increasingly divergent from one another. These expectations were not realized. I did not find Israeli, Canadian, and American memory communities with identifiably different oral traditions of Starachowice. And I did not find that certain topics had become taboo over time in favor of a simpler, less ambiguous narrative. On the contrary, as we shall see in the next chapter, one very sensitive topic was broached more frequently and with greater candor in the later testimonies than earlier. In short, survivor memories proved to be more stable and less malleable than I had anticipated. In this regard I share the counterintuitive conclusion of Henry Greenspan that the lack of difference between early and late survivor testimonies is "most noteworthy and remarkable."[13]

But why Starachowice? Until the movie *Schindler's List* (an obviously untypical case!) on the one hand and the recent restitution settlement for the corporate exploitation of slave labor on the other, the factory slave labor camps were a virtually unexamined phenomenon of the Holocaust. From the Nazi labor camps east of Starachowice, there are virtually no survivors, because these camps were systematically liquidated in 1943. For the factory camps of the Radom district, which survived until their evacuation in the summer of 1944, we have only one scholarly study—Felicja Karay's magnificent but virtually unknown study of the Skarzysko-Kammienna camps, entitled *Death Comes in Yellow*.[14] A study of one such camp complex does not permit wider generalizations. Studies of two will allow us to ascertain both the general characteristics of such camps as well as the particular traits of each. In doing so, it will help us to fill a major lacuna in Holocaust scholarship.

In the remainder of this chapter, I would like to share my construction, based primarily on survivor testimony, of the general history of the Starachowice camps. In the next chapter I would like to switch from a wide-angle to a close-up lens and examine in detail the last seven days of the camp—from the first steps of the evacuation to the arrival of prisoners in Birkenau.

In 1939 some three thousand Jews lived in the old town of Wierzbnik next to the new Polish town of Starachowice, which was the site of steel and munitions factories. In September 1939 the Starachowice factories were expropriated by the Germans and awarded to the industrial conglomerate known as the Hermann Göring Werke.

In the following months, the Jews of nearby Wierzbnik were subjected to an intensifying array of persecutory measures that culminated in the creation of an open, that is nonwalled, ghetto in the spring of 1941. A Jewish council was imposed, and it sought to mitigate German rule in two very typical ways. It organized the allocation of compulsory labor through Jewish officials to replace the capricious and unpredictable terror of arbitrary roundups, in the course of which Jews became an important labor force in the Starachowice factories from which they had been barred employment in the prewar period.[15] And the Jewish council systematically bribed German officials in the hope that they would develop a vested interest in the preservation of the Jewish community.[16]

At the same time the Jewish population of Wierzbnik nearly doubled. A first wave of newcomers came in 1940–41 in the form of transports of Jews expelled from territories of western Poland that had been annexed to the Third Reich and were being demographically transformed through what we now call "ethnic cleansing." The major transports at this time came from Lodz and Plock. Then, as Jewish ghettos in the surrounding towns were being liquidated in 1942, a second influx of Jews from the Radom district flooded into Starachowice in the hope that work in the factories would be their salvation. By the fall of 1942, in short, there were three identifiable groups of Jews in Wierzbnik: the prewar population, the expellees from the west, and finally, the desperate refugees from nearby towns.

Since the summer of 1942, Heinrich Himmler had been pressing for the liquidation of all Polish ghettos by the end of the year. He also adamantly insisted on keeping to an absolute minimum the number of Jewish workers who would be allowed to survive even temporarily. In particular, he insisted on three conditions for corporate users of Jewish labor. First, they had to rent their slaves from the SS at a fixed rate (five zloty per man and four zloty per woman per day). Second, he insisted that they build camps in which to lodge and control their Jewish workers, so that the ghettos could be completely cleared. And third, they were to be engaged in production truly vital to the war economy.[17] The Hermann Göring Werke in Starachowice complied with all three conditions, and this was crucial. Routinely in the Radom district, 90–95 percent of the Jews were deported directly from each ghetto to Treblinka in the three horrific months of August, September, and October 1942. In contrast, when the Wierzbnik ghetto was cleared on October 27, 1942, some 70 percent of the Jews were driven to the loading platform and deported by train to Treblinka, while close to 30 percent of the Jews, about twelve hundred men and four hundred women, were marched from the town square of Wierzbnik to already constructed work camps.[18]

Initially the Wierzbnik Jews were distributed between two large and two small camps. The workers assigned to the munitions factory were lodged in a primitive camp called Strelnica. It had been hastily constructed on a shooting range outside of town and lacked virtually any sanitary facilities. The workers in the steel works were lodged in the marginally less primitive Majowka camp, on the edge of a stone bluff.[19] Smaller contingents of Jews were assigned to the sawmill and lumberyard known as Tartak and, for a brief period, also to the electricity works. In the late summer of 1943, Strelnica was closed down and its prisoners were transferred to the enlarged Majowka camp. Finally, in the late spring or early summer of 1944, Majowka was also closed, and the prisoners were shifted once again to a new camp directly on the grounds of the munitions factory. It was from here that they and the Tartak workers were evacuated to Birkenau on July 28, 1944.

I would like to focus on three aspects of life in the Starachowice camps in the twenty-one months of their existence: first, the trajectory of German policies as reflected in the changing commandants and mortality rates; second, the prisoners' perceptions and categorization of the German perpetrators; and third, the internal governance, underground economy, and social tensions within the camp.

The succession of three commandants mark three distinct periods in the mortality and survival patterns of the main camps: an unmitigated reign of terror and killing under Willi Althoff, a crucial reversal in killing policy that preceded the partial de-escalation of terror under Walter Kolditz, and relative stabilization under Kurt Otto Baumgarten. Willi Althoff was the chief of security of the Starachowice factories and had under his command a force of Ukrainian guards for this purpose. With the construction of the Jewish camps, not unnaturally, Althoff became the first commandant, and the Ukrainians became camp as well as factory guards. A handsome, well-dressed man, who donned a raincoat to keep his clothes from being splattered with blood, Althoff descended upon the main camps, especially Strelnica, virtually every night and left dead Jews in his wake. Many of his killings were theatrically staged for his greater personal amusement and even to entertain guests.[20]

Though Althoff's obvious "pleasure" in killing remained foremost in the memories of the prisoners, it must not obscure the fundamental policy of the factory management that lay behind it. Given the utter lack of sanitary facilities, the Starachowice camps were swept by epidemics, above all typhus. The response of the factory management, quite simply, was not to improve sanitary conditions but rather to kill the sick and weak Jews who would otherwise have cost them five or four zloty per day while not working. The spectacular "amusement" or "entertainment" aspects of his killings aside, the bulk of Althoff's victims were the sick and weak. In addition to conducting notorious running and stair races to select the weak, Althoff twice entered the isolation barracks for typhus patients and killed every single person. On occasion he also searched through the barracks to discover and shoot sick prisoners in their beds.[21] And on at least one and possibly two occasions, large numbers of prisoners were selected, put on trucks, driven to the nearby Bugaj forest, shot, and buried in a mass grave. Polish workers reported to Jewish workers in the factories that for days the earth over the grave moved—an image that still haunted many survivor memories years later and is probably the source of recurring references in the Starachowice testimonies to the Germans burying people alive.[22]

By May 1943 the Germans had completed a second sweep of what they called the "remnant" ghettos in central Poland. In the Radom district there were virtually no Jews still alive who were not either hiding or in work camps. Jewish labor had become a scarce commodity, which altered economic calculations entirely. Jews who had been killed could not be replaced, but sick Jews—despite the expense of paying the SS for them while they were unproductive—could still recover and return to work. This simple fact was reflected in an abrupt change in factory management policy. Althoff was suddenly sent away, and the factory management announced that henceforth sick prisoners would no longer be shot.[23]

Althoff's eventual successor as commandant was the extremely obese Walter Kolditz. He closed the notorious Strelnica camp, which had been Althoff's chief killing site, and moved the prisoners from there to the newly enlarged and slightly less unsanitary Majowka camp.[24] While killing was no longer an "everyday" event, the Kolditz era was marked by at least one extremely sadistic killing on the one hand[25] and the most lethal single selection in the camps' history on the other. On November 3–4, 1943, the Germans had carried out the notorious Erntefest or "Fall Harvest" massacre in the neighboring Lublin district. In two days they murdered over forty-two thousand prisoners and liquidated all but two small work camps in the entire district. These Lublin camps had been under direct SS control. The factory work camps of the Radom district did not suffer the same fate. Nevertheless, many of the Radom camps, including Starachowice, were subjected to a major selection just days later. On November 8, 1943, some 150–160 Jews were selected and taken by truck not to the nearby Bugaj forest as in previous selections but rather to Firlej near Radom. Here, alongside victims from other camps, they were killed by SS executioners.[26] Both timing and manner of execution would suggest that this selection was imposed by the SS as a districtwide policy and was not the result of a local initiative by either factory management or Kolditz.

Sometime after the Firlej selection, Kolditz was relieved of his duties and replaced as commandant by Kurt Otto Baumgarten, hitherto a division manager within the munitions factory. Individual killings continued within the camp, though in each case for some identifiable cause. There is no testimony about any "amusement" killing during the Baumgarten era. The largest execution was the "hostage" shooting of ten prisoners from the blast furnace work force, as punishment and deterrent for the successful mass escape of ten coworkers.[27] The primary killers for this period were the chief of the Ukrainian guard, Willi Schroth, and one of the deputies of factory security, Gerhard Kaschmieder.

One of the unusual features of the collected memories of the Starachowice survivors is that 116 of the testimonies were taken by German judicial investigators seeking evidence about specific crimes and suspected perpetrators. Prosecution for murder under the German criminal code required evidence concerning the "malicious" or "cruel" manner in which the crimes were committed or the "base motives" behind the crimes. Thus, far more than in any other form of survivor testimony, this particular collection of testimonies offers a concentrated focus from the perspective of the victims on both the behavior as well as attitudes and mind-set of the German personnel in Starachowice. For the prisoners, the ability to distinguish between German perpetrators was one key to survival.

Aside from the many nondescript Germans whose behavior did not imprint itself on survivor memory, three rough categories of Germans emerge. The first category was composed of what the survivors referred to as the "dangerous" Germans, such as Althoff, who killed often and with personal zeal and pleasure. The second category was composed of "corrupt" Germans. These were men who were susceptible to bribes and with whom negotiations were undertaken and businesslike deals were made. The prime examples here were the chief of personnel, Leopold Schwertner, and the last commandant, Kurt Otto Baumgarten. Before the liquidation of the ghetto, Schwertner was notorious for selling work cards to individual Jews, touring nearby towns to pick up Jewish workers by the truckload in return for money, as well as for taking payments from the Jewish council to create as many new jobs for Jews as possible.[28] Eventually Jewish valuables were found in Schwertner's apartment, and he was arrested for corruption. After a few months he was released from prison but banned from the occupied territories, because he was deemed "not suited for responsible assignments in the east."[29]

During the camp period, the focal point of bribes and negotiations was Baumgarten. Among the survivors, Baumgarten was remembered both for his costume—leather Bavarian shorts and suspenders and Tyrolean hat—and for his insatiable greed.[30] At least some testimony hints that Baumgarten played a role in the removal of Althoff and Kolditz.[31] In his dual capacity as both a manager within the munitions plant and commandant of the Jewish labor camps, Baumgarten strove to increase corporate production and profits as well as line his own pockets. Both goals were best served by negotiating with and extorting rather than killing his Jewish workers.

In addition to the "dangerous" and "corrupt" Germans, the third and certainly smallest category was that of the "decent" Germans, with whom Jewish prisoners found refuge and protection. Most remarkable in this regard were a man named Fiedler (in some accounts Fickler), who had taken over the Jewish-owned sawmill and lumberyard, and his deputy Piatek.[32] Together they presided over the Tartak camp, which produced munitions crates and other wood products for the German military. Jews in the Tartak camp were not only better clothed and fed, they were above all more secure. Fiedler personally assured them that nothing would happen to them as long as he was there.[33] Indeed the camp had no guards, for prisoners were not trying to escape from Tartak. On the contrary, they paid to get themselves or their relatives transferred there.[34] Quite simply, there was no place in this area of Poland that was safer for Jews.

Let us turn our attention now from German policies and personnel to the prisoner society within the Starachowice camps. As already noted, the original prisoners were already divided into three groups based upon a kind of seniority: the prewar Wierzbnikers, the early refugees from western Poland (especially Lodz and Plock), and the late wave of refugees from nearby communities. Once interned, the camp population was constantly suffering attrition from executions and epidemics but also replenished by the transfer of additional prisoners. Most came from other camps in the Radom district, and in particular, a large contingent came from Wolanow when the labor camp there was closed down. There were also large contingents from Radom, Plaszow, and Tomaszowa. Most conspicuous, however, was a group of some two hundred Jews who arrived in Starachowice via the camps of Majdanek and Budzyn in the Lublin district. Wearing uniforms marked with the large letters *KL* for "Konzentrationslager," they were referred to as the "KLs" or "Lubliners."

If geographical origin and date of arrival in Starachowice were two key factors in creating the groups that clung together and thus in shaping the social hierarchy within the prisoner community, the third key factor affecting the nature of camp society was the continuing existence of family ties. For both Starachowice and other camps like Wolanow that eventually fed into Starachowice, the purchase of work permits had usually been a family strategy for survival. Many immediate families entered Starachowice intact, others at least partially intact. Though men and women lived in separate barracks, considerable contact was possible, especially in the post-Althoff era.[35] And as typhus swept through the camps, eventually affecting virtually every prisoner, family members who cared for and nursed one another as they fell ill in sequence were crucial for survival.

And some families who had placed in hiding those children too young for work permits reunified their families by eventually smuggling their children into the camp. After the Althoff reign of terror was past, they calculated the risk of their children trying to survive in hiding to be greater than trying to live as an "illegal" child in camp.[36] Thus one unusual characteristic of the Starachowice camps was the presence of children, not only a number of "illegal" children who had been smuggled into camp in one way or another but also the "legal" children of the privileged. One very positive aspect of the latter, of course, was that it made the presence of the former less conspicuous. Indeed, some of the "illegal" children testified to having been placed with the "legal" children during searches and selections.[37]

In no German camps, needless to say, was prisoner life organized on egalitarian and democratic principles. On the contrary, the infamous kapo system of divide and control through granting internal power and privilege to some prisoners at the expense of others was the norm everywhere. Starachowice was no exception in this regard.

At the top of the camp hierarchy stood the Wierzbniker Jeremiah Wilczek, surrounded by a coterie of family, relatives, and supporters, as well as three members of the now disbanded Wierzbnik Jewish council. This group controlled the camp council, camp police, and camp kitchen. The camp elite enjoyed a number of privileges that the other prisoners did not. They lived in separate housing with their wives and in some cases with their children whom they had been allowed to bring into camp.[38] They were also able to maintain contact with people outside the camp and even visit them in town, in order to conduct business or have access to valuables hidden with friends.[39] In numerous testimonies Wilczek and the camp elite were also accused of living and eating well, in effect stealing from the common food and clothing supply while the rest of the camp suffered hunger and dressed in rags.[40] Two testimonies lodge the even more serious charge that Wilczek and the camp council participated in the selections, in effect helping the Germans decide who would live and who would die.[41]

Although no testimonies praised either Wilczek or the camp police as a whole, some explicitly credited the intervention of individual policemen with saving their lives.[42] Indeed, only one policeman, Szaja Langsleben, was uniformly condemned in every account that mentioned him.[43] But one pattern is clear. Most disenchanted with the camp council and hierarchy of privilege were latecomers to the camp from outside Starachowice. When prisoners from the Wolanow camp near Radom, where the Jewish camp leaders had imposed a strict but relatively honest and egalitarian regime, were transferred to Starachowice in 1943, they were dismayed by the rampant inequality and abuse of power they encountered. The newcomers' possessions were taken from them under the guise of disinfection; these possessions were never returned but instead sold to Poles on the black market. Rare items like meat and sugar that they had received occasionally at Wolanow were in Starachowice sold to those who could pay, with the camp council pocketing the proceeds. When Wolanow newcomers protested indignantly, they were branded as rebels, discriminated against even more in terms of being assigned the worst jobs, and dispersed among different barracks so they could not act in concert. The new arrivals from Tomasjowa and Majdanek were likewise deprived of their possessions.[44]

The greatest challenge to the camp elite was posed by the two hundred hardened survivors of Majdanek and Budzyn, who arrived in Starachowice in the spring of 1944. The so-called Lubliners openly challenged the Starachowice elite for control of the camp and temporarily placed one of their own as chairman of the camp council. Thereupon the old camp elite apparently paid even greater sums to Baumgarten and bribed its way back into power, though it was careful thereafter not to flaunt its privilege quite so openly.[45] To some of the prisoners, the Lubliners were tough veterans of the SS camp system, who were "made out of iron."[46] To others they were low-class thugs grasping for power.[47] In any case, the deep animosity between the Wilczek coterie and the Lubliners remained unabated.

The vital role that Baumgarten's corruption and greed played in the camp's history raises, of course, the question as to how such large-scale, systemic bribery could be financed? Within Starachowice, as in other camps, virtually every prisoner sought to "organize" materials from the work site that could be made into marketable goods. In Starachowice, such goods were traded at the work site or smuggled out of camp when the more well disposed of the Ukrainian guards were on duty and sold to Poles on the black market.[48] Much of this income then flowed to the camp council through the purchase of both extra food and preferred work assignments.[49] But beyond such income coming from individual prisoner initiative, there was an underground camp economy of considerable complexity that enabled the camp council to finance the crucial network of bribery. Within the camp the Germans had collected a group of skilled craftsmen, such as tailors and shoemakers, to work for them. This craftsmen's center was know as the Konsum. In addition to working for the Germans, it also worked for the camp council, which provided it with raw materials and sold the resulting goods. For instance, when a shipment of two thousand pair of shoes was sent from Majdanek to Starachowice, the camp council distributed only one hundred pairs to the ill-shod prisoners. The rest were cut up, and the craftsmen used the materials to make tops for wooden-soled shoes that were sold on the black market.[50]

But the most unusual feature of the Starachowice underground economy, and the one that gave decisive advantage in the internal dynamics of the camp society, owed to the fact that the original Wierzbnikers were still in their hometown. Not just the wealthier and more assimilated families, with whom Wilczek was allied, but even many ordinary Wierzbnikers had had both business and social contacts in the Polish community with whom they had left property. On some occasions they were permitted to go into town to conduct business and retrieve valuables; on other occasions money was smuggled into camp from local sources.[51] This was a resource that none of the subsequent waves of Jews that came into the Starachowice camps could match.[52]

Overall, how did the Starachowice camps compare with the survivors' other experiences within the universe of the German camp system? Notoriously, in comparison of other camps, those of Starachowice were the filthiest, most lice- and bug-infested camps, with the highest incidence of typhus, of any. Alongside Starachowice, Auschwitz was a model of cleanliness. Work at the factories was physically debilitating, the production quotas unremitting and ever increasing, and the conditions terrible. In the blast furnace of the steel mill in particular, the heat was excruciating. The food was poor in quality and inadequate in quantity. Though malnourished, however, the prisoners did not perish from mass starvation. Once in Auschwitz, many of them noted that the Jews arriving from Lodz were clearly more emaciated and physically broken. If Althoff was viewed by many survivors as the most crazed and dangerous German they had encountered in the entire camp system, the Starachowice camp regime of the post-Althoff period was less fearful than those of their subsequent experiences.

Most unusual for Starachowice camps was the convergence of fortuitous factors, by virtue of which we have 173 survivor testimonies that make it possible to write their history. First, some 30 percent of the Jews in Wierzbnik were taken into the camps, and "only" 70 percent were sent directly to Treblinka when the ghetto was liquidated. Second, the Starachowice camps were not transferred to direct SS control but remained under factory management. This permitted economic calculation temporarily to mitigate the exhortations of Heinrich Himmler and the imperatives of Nazi ideology. The murderous attrition of the Starachowice prisoners was crucially moderated and curtailed in the spring of 1943. Third, the systematic liquidation of the labor camps that swept through the German-occupied east, and especially the districts of Galicia and Lublin in the summer and fall of 1943, stopped just short of the factory camps of the Radom district. In fact Starachowice was at the eastern edge of the surviving camps. And fourth, in late July 1944 the Starachowice Jews were evacuated and brought into Birkenau in mass without the usual decimating selection. It is the final days of the Starachowice camps— the evacuation and arrival in Birkenau—that we will examine in detail in the following chapter.

3

Survivor Testimonies
from Starachowice

The Final Days

In the previous chapter I argued that the collected survivor testimonies of the Starachowice factory slave labor camps allow the historian reliably to reconstruct the general course of events over the twenty-one months of the camps' existence. Moreover, these testimonies enable the historian to analyze the internal governance and underground economy, to dissect the internal tensions and divisions within the prisoner community, and to portray the key characteristics of and differences among the major German perpetrators as well as shifting German policy. Now I would like to shift focus from these broad subjects and take a detailed look at one crucial week in the life of the Starachowice prisoners. This is the last week in July 1944, from the point at which they learned of the assassination attempt on Hitler and heard the distant sound of approaching Soviet artillery to their evacuation from the camp and arrival in Auschwitz-Birkenau.

Some time earlier the prisoners had already been moved from the camp at Majowka to a new camp directly adjacent to the munitions factory for shell production. This relocation was a response to the increasingly brazen partisan attacks on the guards marching the prisoners to work.[1] These attacks had been aimed, of course, not at liberating the prisoners but at seizing weapons from the Ukrainian guards, who had become increasingly uninterested in fighting. Work at the factories shifted from producing munitions to dismantling equipment, which clearly signaled the end of the camp in the not-too-distant future.[2] When some of the Lubliners, who upon their arrival that spring had already confirmed the existence of gas chambers, recognized Majdanek personnel among a visiting SS commission, the sense of panic intensified among the prisoners.[3] The sound of distant artillery and the approach of the Red Army raised the imminent prospect that the prisoners would be either shot in mass before liberation or evacuated to an unknown camp and unknown fate.

The first concrete step taken by the Germans to close the Starachowice camps came with the evacuation of the Tartak sawmill and lumberyard. The manager of this camp, Fiedler, had previously assured the prisoners that nothing would happen to them as long as he was there. According to Josef K. he had added, "If he were to leave, we could do as we wanted. In this regard he always referred to the lack of any guard." Then one day he left camp abruptly. One-half hour later a truck with Ukrainian guards was seen approaching the camp. Some prisoners, particularly young ones who knew the city, tried to jump the stream running behind the camp and escape. Some managed to get away but others were shot down. The sawmill and lumberyard were quickly surrounded, and the Jews were ordered to assemble for evacuation to the main camp. To the astonishment of Josef K., some Jews had already armed themselves with axes and knives and, fearing transport to an extermination camp, were prepared to fight to the death. Josef K. advised against resistance, arguing that in the main camp they would know better what was going on. And resistance there with greater numbers was possible, while in the sawmill it was hopeless. Most of the prisoners agreed with him and mounted two canopy-covered trucks. Some still tried to escape, but only a few made it.[4]

After the Jews from the lumberyard were unloaded at the main camp that evening, a dramatic event occurred that was mentioned in no less than eleven testimonies. I would like to examine the testimony concerning this incident in detail to illustrate the challenges and opportunities in using such evidence. The earliest testimony of the entire collection, by Mendel K., is a long, detailed account, recorded in Cracow and dated August 21, 1945. According to Mendel K., when the prisoners from Tartak were separated into men and women, a young twenty-year-old girl attacked the head of the camp guard and pushed him to the ground. He freed himself from her grasp, drew his revolver and shot her in the forehead. In fact the bullet just grazed her, but she faked being dead. After the guards left, she crawled under the barracks to hide. The next morning the commander of the guards returned and, not finding the body, searched for her. She then gave herself up.[5] This account does not tell us anything further about the fate of the girl.

Nearly one year later, on July 31, 1946, in France, the eighteen-year-old Kalman E. gave an interview to David Boder that was audio-recorded and subsequently transcribed.[6] Kalman E. testified that when the Jews from the small camps were brought into the main camp, a young girl originally from Lodz called out: "Jews, time now counts in minutes. Perhaps we will be able to escape. And whoever dies will die a hero's death." She then threw herself on the German commander of the Ukrainian guard, seized his revolver, and fired into the air. The guards ran up and fired on the Jewish prisoners. Because it was very dark, no one was killed. The girl was only slightly wounded and able to hide in the barracks. In the morning she was dragged out of the barracks and taken to interrogation, where she defended herself.

Kalman E. then stated that "with great difficulty, with much labor and struggle, we succeeded in saving the girl from death." When the incredulous Boder asked how this had been accomplished, Kalman E. explained: "It has cost us very much money. The Jews gave up their last possessions." He went on to explain how Jews from Starachowice had left possessions with Poles, and some of this property was later transferred into the camp when Polish and Jewish workers met at the factories. Because the camp commandant "was a big glutton for money" and "loved money and gold very much," the Jews had handed over their possessions and the girl was saved.[7] In short, the Jewish prisoners had negotiated with the commandant and ransomed her release at a high price.

The final early testimony of Josef K. was given two years later, on August 19, 1948, in Germany. He stated that it was dark when the Jews from Tartak arrived at the main camp. From the Appellplatz they were taken away in groups of ten by Ukrainian guards. They feared that they were about to be shot. In one group of ten, a young woman threw herself on the commander of the Ukrainians, Willi Schroth (whom he called "Schrutt"), and began to strangle him in desperation, while calling upon the other Jews to attack the Ukrainian guards. "But no one moved. We were as if paralyzed," he recalled. Then suddenly the air raid alarm sounded, and the lights went out. Schroth threw the women off, pulled his revolver, and shot her twice. Everyone assumed she was dead. When the German police chief Becker ("Beck" in his version) came the next morning, she had disappeared and no one would betray her. But fearful that others would suffer, the "brave girl" gave herself up. When asked why she had done it, she answered that she feared being shot and in her fear had fallen on Schroth, which he had mistakenly thought was an attack. At this moment, Josef K. surmised, Becker was more concerned about a general uprising of the prisoners and knew the Jews were all going to Auschwitz anyway. Thus he proclaimed that if two bullets had not killed her, she would not be killed on his orders, and the girl survived.[8]

In short, in three early accounts given in three different countries, the same incident is recounted of a young female prisoner attacking the head of the Ukrainian camp guards at the moment the Jews of Tartak were brought into the main camp. Otherwise they differ in important ways. Only two of the accounts note that the attacker was spared, and they in turn give two different explanations for the very unusual behavior of the Germans in this regard. These two accounts also differ on the identification of the man who made the decision to spare the women. Kalman E.'s description refers to the insatiably greedy camp commandant, presumably Baumgarten, while Josef K. names Becker, the head of the German police in Starachowice. Only the third account identified the commander of the camp guards, Schroth, by name.

Three additional testimonies taken in 1966 and 1967 by German judicial investigators also describe the incident. All three were female friends of the attacker, whom they identified as Guta B. Otherwise their accounts differ. According to the first account, after the Tartak prisoners had been moved to the main camp, Guta argued with Schroth. He pulled his pistol and shot her. She fell. He kicked her and then drove the other prisoners into the barracks. They all thought that she was dead, but she crawled into the barracks and was hidden and saved. In short, in this version Guta confronted Schroth verbally but there was no physical attack, and she was saved by fellow prisoners who hid her, not by the decision of any German.[9] In the second account, Guta tried to strangle not Schroth but Becker, who shot her and left her for dead. Only wounded, she crawled to the barracks and survived.[10] In the third account, the witness and four others had been taken out from the group and were about to be shot by Schroth. He was running back and forth in front of them with pistol drawn, when

Guta leapt on his back. In the ensuing struggle he shot her in the leg and left her for dead. But when he returned in the morning, the body was gone, and he demanded that she be turned over. However, her life was saved when another man in uniform intervened and declared that she was "too brave" to be shot.[11]

Four late testimonies also mention the incident. One witness, in an audiotaped interview in 1986, recalled that the night the lumberyard prisoners had been taken to the main camp by truck, one woman attacked Schroth, who shot her. She pretended to be dead and then crawled under the barrack. The next day, when the Germans could not find the body, the prisoners bribed Schroth to spare her.[12] A second witness account of 1988 related how, after the lumberyard prisoners had been taken to the main camp, the Germans got pleasure and enjoyment from scaring them. They separated the men and women and took people off into the dark. One strong woman then jumped on a small German soldier and almost choked him. After that the Germans did not play games anymore but took the prisoners to their barracks. Amazingly, the woman was shot but not killed, and by an unexplained "miracle," the commandant let the woman live.[13] In a personal interview in 2001, another witness confirmed that Guta, a beautiful young woman, had jumped on Schroth on the evening the Tartak prisoners were being unloaded at the main camp. Schroth shot her, but she survived and hid. It was Baumgarten who arrived the next day and spared her.[14]

The tenth and eleventh versions of this incident are those of Guta B. herself. She was interviewed by German investigators in 1968, but at that point they were solely interested in her as a potential witness in the impending Becker trial. Whatever she may have said about her overall experiences, nothing was recorded in the protocol about this incident involving Schroth and Baumgarten.[15] Subsequently she gave an audiotaped interview in 1984 that is in the Museum of Jewish Heritage and then a videotaped interview for the United States Holocaust Memorial Museum in

1990.[16] She described the incident in question in both interviews, but added further details to the second account. In her first account, upon entering the main camp, the prisoners from Tartak were made to line up in front of two long graves, and Schroth told them they had one minute to pray, then they would be shot. Thinking especially of her mother who had turned pale, she ran out and jumped on Schroth's back, wrapped her legs around him, and dug her fingernails into his throat. Fearful of hitting him, the other guards did not shoot but eventually pulled them apart. Schroth did not shoot her immediately but wanted to make her dance first. She remained limp, and Schroth then shot her, grazing her forehead. At that point Russian planes approached to bomb nearby targets, and the Germans ran for cover. The searchlights went out, and Guta crawled under the barracks and was subsequently hidden by her parents. When Schroth could not find her body the following morning, he threatened to shoot everyone, so she gave herself up. She was locked in a room and then interrogated by the (unnamed) camp commandant who demanded to know why she had attacked a German officer. She told him that she had only approached Schroth to beg for their lives but could remember nothing thereafter due to her head injuries. She was then released when her boyfriend and future husband gave the commandant a diamond that he had successfully kept hidden.

In her second account she repeated the story that they were lined up by a long grave and told they would be shot in one minute. She added that several weeks earlier a drunken Schroth had made sexual advances toward her, which she had barely evaded. She also noted that after receiving the diamond, Baumgarten took her first to the camp infirmary for bandaging and then returned her to the barracks.

Given the number of concurring accounts, I think that we can conclude beyond any reasonable doubt that Guta B. attacked the head of the Ukrainian camp guard, Willi Schroth, shortly after the Tartak prisoners arrived at the main camp, was shot in the head at point-blank range, and remarkably survived both this shooting and expected German retribution. The preponderance of evidence suggests that Baumgarten was the man who made the decision to spare her life. Among the competing explanations—a "miracle," German respect for her heroism, hiding, and bribery— once again the preponderance of evidence suggests bribery as Baumgarten's key motive. Baumgarten was notorious for his corruption, and this was his final chance to extort one last payoff from his Jewish prisoners.

More problematic are the points at which Guta B.'s own testimony differs from that of other witnesses. Quite simply, her undoubted heroism at the age of eighteen is no surety of an infallible memory nearly fifty years later. I think that she incorporated into her own memory the now archetypal Holocaust image of Jews lined up at the edge of a mass grave about to be shot. No other witness mentions a mass grave or mass executions inside the camp at this time, and the Germans as a rule did not carry out those kinds of executions within camp boundaries. The accounts of two other witnesses that the guards were tormenting and scaring the prisoners rather than preparing an actual execution are more probable than Guta's version.

The motive she gives for attacking Schroth in this setting was to save her parents' lives from an imminent execution, which in fact did not take place. According to Kalman E.'s account, Guta called upon her fellow prisoners to attempt to escape. According to Josef K., she urged them to attack the guards but the other Jews remained paralyzed as she struggled with Schroth. Again, within the context of the failure of most of the Tartak prisoners to escape when Fiedler departed, an attempt by Guta to make up for this lost opportunity and instigate a mass escape upon arrival at the main camp has a contextual plausibility. In this case, her heroic attack on Schroth was not a miraculous success that saved the lives of her parents, as she remembered it, but rather a suicidal risk that failed to inspire any commensurate action among her fellow prisoners.

Finally, Guta remembers her rescue as due to the single-handed action of her boyfriend and future husband, who purchased her life with a diamond. The other two witnesses who account for her rescue through bribery remember a collective action. There is no reason to doubt that her boyfriend contributed a diamond to the ransom, but once again a larger ransom collected from numerous prisoners and negotiated through those who had experience in dealing with Baumgarten seems more plausible.

If my reconstruction is correct, then this episode has a twofold significance. First, it was a singular act of resistance, in which an unarmed eighteen-year-old woman risked a virtually suicidal attack on the head of the camp guard in order to give her fellow prisoners a last chance to escape but nonetheless survived. Second, on the eve of the evacuation of the camp, every prisoner must have been sorely tempted to husband his or her hidden valuables to increase the chances of survival in the face of a tremendously uncertain future. Instead, in an act of solidarity and collective endeavor, a number of prisoners pooled their resources to purchase the life of a fellow prisoner. The camp system was of course designed to not only divide prisoners but also pit them one against the other in a Darwinian struggle to survive. Numerous survivor accounts confirm the seemingly inexorable logic of the zero-sum game, in which one prisoner's gain could come only at the price of another prisoner's loss. But the cruel logic of the zero-sum game did not always prevail. In this case Guta B. attempted to sacrifice herself to save her fellow prisoners. In the end, it was they who sacrificed to save her.

In trying to reconstruct not only the correct sequence but also the actual dates of events during the last week of the camp, the historian is faced with two difficulties. First, most survivors made no attempt to fit their memories into a precise chronological narrative much less provide precise dating. Second, those who did so invariably offer somewhat conflicting sequences. In short, my attempt not only to place events in a particular sequence but to space and date them precisely is a hazardous venture at best. The beginning point must be the one date that seems to be reliably fixed, namely that the numbers with which the Starachowice survivors were tattooed upon arrival in Birkenau were assigned to prisoners on a transport from the Radom district that arrived on Sunday, July 30.[17] This is according to the Auschwitz *Kalendarium*. But even this date is not uncontested. The Kalendarium is not without dating errors, and one survivor distinctly remembers arriving in Birkenau on his birthday, July 31.[18]

Working backwards, it is my best estimate that the prisoners of the sawmill and lumberyard had been brought into the main camp on the evening of Monday, July 24, and Guta B.'s life was ransomed from Baumgarten the next day, Tuesday, July 25. On Wednesday, July 26, the many rumors of impending evacuation were confirmed. A train arrived at the factory, and loading began. Then, mysteriously, the action was stopped. Those who had already been loaded were unloaded, and the prisoners were herded back into the factory camp. No explanation was given.[19]

For some time prisoners had known the end was near. As one put it, a "feeling of doom" hung over the camp.[20] A Jewish resistance organization on the outside had been urging prisoners to attempt an escape. Some prisoners were in the process of obtaining false identification papers with photographs, but the documents had not yet arrived.[21] Now there was clearly no time left, and some prisoners who were determined to attempt an escape resolved to make their bid that night. On this issue, apparently, a split occurred within the camp police. The much-hated Szaja Langsleben had emerged as the chief enforcer on behalf of the Germans for a stricter control within the camp, but other policeman were now ready not only to join but even to lead the escape attempt.[22] In two accounts the policeman Moshe Herblum took the lead in organizing it.[23] By another account, the policeman Abraham Wilczek was the leader.[24] In yet a third account, a man named Wajgenszperg took the lead.[25] Most plausibly, the leadership was collective, and at least several policemen were deeply involved.

Several hundred prisoners in a camp of nearly two thousand intended to take part in the breakout. Many were not even aware of the impending attempt, as news had of course to be spread by word of mouth. Some were not invited. For instance, Esther K.'s brother came to her, gave her his bread, and said goodnight without saying a word of his impending escape attempt.[26] Others knew but decided against taking part. Many were dissuaded by pleas of family members.[27] Others calculated the risk as too high. Joseph Z. from Plock decided against an attempt because he did not know the territory.[28] Joseph T. feared that if he tried to hide in town, he would be turned over to the Germans, and if he went to the forest, he would be killed by partisans. After all, he noted, if there had been any place to go, he could have escaped from the factory at any time.[29] Ironically, those with the best knowledge of local terrain were most likely to be impeded by fears of deserting their families, while those in camp without any family ties were the outsiders and latecomers least likely to feel confident about escaping into unknown terrain.

Of the 173 surviving witnesses, only fifteen testified about their attempt to take part in the escape.[30] It should be kept in mind, however, that some of those interviewed by German judicial investigators may well have participated but this part of their testimony may have been deemed irrelevant to judicial purposes and therefore was simply not recorded in this major collection of testimonies. In short, participation may have been underrecorded in my overall collection.

The factory camp was surrounded by two fences, the first of wire and the second of wood with wire on top.[31] The plan was simple. According to no fewer than eight accounts, all based on hearsay and not direct participation in the transaction, contact was made with Polish partisans, who were to shoot out the search-lights. In one such hearsay account, a half million zlotys had been paid in advance for this service, with another half million promised afterwards.[32] An initial group, armed with wire cutters and axes, was then to make an opening in the fence. A second and third group were ready to rush through, while many others hid under barracks and watched for their chance to join.

The Jews waited through the night for the partisans to shoot out the searchlights. But they never came, which is remembered by a number of the survivors as an act of Polish betrayal or deception. Suddenly the lights went off anyway, perhaps due to a nearby air raid. The first group ran for the first fence, cut through the wire, and then began pulling away boards from the second fence, which made a great deal of noise.[33] Overcrowding at the fence led to panic, and some of the more agile Jews tried to climb the fence instead of waiting for an opening to be made.[34] The Ukrainian guards were alerted by the commotion, turned on the searchlights, and opened fire. Henry G. was with his sister and the policeman, Moshe Herblum, and was apparently one of the first to be hit. He suffered a head wound, briefly lost consciousness, and then fled back to the women's barracks, where a cousin bandaged his head wound.[35] The initial fire from the towers did not halt the escape attempt. However, the head of the Ukrainian guard, Schroth, arrived on the scene and tossed a hand grenade into the opening that had been made in the fence with devastating effect. Schroth then moved a machine gun into position and opened fire, and the ensuing massacre of the first group was virtually complete.[36] Those who were already through the first wire and were now caught between the two fences tried desperately to get back into the camp and hide.[37] Many others who had been still waiting their chance to join the breakout gave up any attempt in the face of the hand grenade explosion and machine-gun fire.[38]

The following morning, Thursday, July 27, the prisoners were assembled and counted to establish how many were missing. They were marched past the wire where a number of prisoners (in one estimate, twenty to thirty) lay badly wounded and were begging to be either helped or shot. But Schroth prohibited any help from being given; the wounded and dead were to be left for the dogs to eat, he proclaimed.[39] Henry G. saw that his sister, the last surviving member of his family in addition to himself, had died—"in freedom" as he put it—just several feet beyond the last fence. Next to her sat the policeman Moshe Herblum, groaning with a terrible stomach wound.[40]

According to two witnesses, sixty-four prisoners were killed in the escape attempt.[41] While trying to account for the missing, Schroth approached Ida G. and asked where her brother-in-law Mayer was. She did not know, and he told her that her brother-in-law was not among the dead. It turned out that he was among the seven that escaped that night, four of whom were captured and killed almost immediately.[42] In a classic example of the frustration in using oral testimony for dating, while both Adam G. and his wife Ida told the same story concerning Mayer G.'s escape in the nighttime breakout attempt in late July, Mayer himself dated the breakout attempt and his escape to April or May of 1944.[43]

According to most accounts, Baumgarten, very possibly accompanied by the police chief Becker, then arrived at the camp. Though some accounts named Becker, most witnesses stated that it was Baumgarten who assembled prisoners and attempted to give them a reassuring and calming, even "friendly," speech. He was "disappointed" with them for the escape attempt, since he had been so good to them. They were indeed going to be sent to another but better camp, with hot and cold running water. They had nothing to fear, for they were the best workers and much needed. He could not understand how they had gotten such an idea that they had to flee, but he blamed the camp police for instigating panic. He then had Moshe Herblum shot as a warning and deterrent.[44] In one account Baumgarten displayed "a certain degree of humanity." Although he had the order to shoot many more, he only had shot a few of the wounded, specifically those who would not have survived in any case.[45]

Even as Baumgarten spoke and continuing after, a number of prisoners made further escape attempts in broad daylight.[46] Rather than attempting a mass breakout through making an opening in the fence, small groups as well as individuals rushed the fence at different points and either scaled it or slithered under it. Others tried but could not make it. The sixteen-year-old Abramek N., who had been wounded in the leg in the breakout attempt the night before, discovered he was too short to get over the fence.[47] Several others got through at least the first fence but ran back into the camp when they encountered approaching guards or were fired upon.[48] But at least two groups, if not more, reached the forest and made good their escape.[49] Once again, among those participating in the escape were prominent members of the camp elite. The policemen, Abraham Wilczek and Szmuel Szczeslewi, and Mendel Mincberg, the son of the former head of the Jewish council, were among those who got away.[50] Shlomo Enesman, a prominent member of first the Judenrat and then the camp council, and his son were not so fortunate. They were both killed in an escape attempt.[51]

The Germans reacted to this flurry of breakout attempts in two ways. First, they increased the guard. Among the reinforcements were military police *(Feldgendarmerie)*, whom the prisoners referred to as "canary birds" because of the yellow stripes on their uniforms.[52] Second, they collected all the prisoners' shoes and outer clothing, in the hope that the Jews would not attempt escape barefoot and half-naked.[53] Among at least a few of the Jewish prisoners, there was a reaction of a different sort. Mistrustful of the camp council and fearing that the camp elite was about to bribe its way out at the last moment, leaving the other prisoners behind to face German reprisal, they put the remaining camp leaders under watch.[54] There were in fact no further large-scale breakout attempts, though several women apparently still managed to slip out of the camp that night and join other escapees in the forest.[55]

On Friday, July 28,[56] the Starachowice prisoners were allowed to reclaim their shoes and clothes.[57] Rachel P. recalls the devastating effect on her father's morale when someone took the opportunity to steal his treasured pair before he could find them, leaving him with wooden clogs. Unable to walk in them, he felt stripped of his dignity and manhood.[58] In the now heavily guarded camp, machine guns had been set up between the two fences.[59] They were trained on the prisoners, who were assembled and left standing in the hot July sun for hours.[60] Some prisoners had dug burrows under barracks in a desperate attempt to hide and evade the evacuation of the camp. When such underground hiding places were discovered, the guards threw hand grenades or shot into the bunkers.[61]

Josef K. approached one of the newly arrived SS guards and asked him outright if they were going to be gassed. At first the guard said that talk of gassing was "quatsch," all the Jews were still alive. When Josef K. pursued the conversation further, the guard finally assured him that while the older ones had to fear death, those capable of work would surely be left alive.[62]

A train then arrived on the track that led directly into the factory grounds and loading began. Most witnesses remember the chief of police, Becker, as the man in charge of the loading, though as in almost every such case, at least some named Baumgarten, Schroth, or even the long-departed Kolditz instead.[63] Such conflicting memory in multiple testimonies may be accepted by the historian as natural and inevitable, but it was especially frustrating to the German judicial investigators who were thereby precluded from including the lethal consequences of the overloading from becoming a point of indictment against Becker later. What is not in any doubt is that most of the train's closed freight cars were terribly overloaded. The women were loaded in different cars from the men. While most were filled so tightly that no one could sit or move about, at least the last women's car had only seventy-five people in it.[64] But the men's cars were packed with one hundred to one hundred fifty persons each.[65] When it proved physically impossible to pack them any tighter, several open cars were brought in and added to the end of the train.[66]

The distance from Starachowice to Auschwitz is less than 140 miles by rail. Stopping for priority trains, the transport apparently took about thirty-six hours, leaving around sunset on Friday night and arriving still in the dark early Sunday morning. Not surprising, survivors offered widely varying estimates of how long the trip lasted, and virtually every survivor remembers it as having taken much longer than it actually did, often estimating three or four days. As one survivor observed, whatever the actual time, it "seemed like an eternity."[67] But if their memories of the length of the journey vary, their memories of the horrific conditions are virtually uniform. They traveled without food or water, or at best with one bucket of water and an additional bucket for human waste. But the cars were packed too tight to get to the latter in any case. It was a sunny late July, and the heat within the closed cars was absolutely stifling. Above all, with just two tiny windows in each car, the prisoners gasped for air in the suffocating stench and heat.

In several of the women's cars there was panic and hysteria.[68] There were also some deaths, especially among the children.[69] Only one woman survivor remembers Poles bringing water to her car at one stop.[70] But another woman survivor told a more unusual story concerning the delivery of water to at least one car. Anna W., who had worked in the camp office before the evacuation, had been approached by one of the military policeman or "canary birds" searching for an envelope. Anna, from a relatively well-to-do family, had been the only Jewish girl from Starachowice to be admitted to a private high school in Radom, where she had studied French. As the military policeman spoke with a French accent, Anna conversed with him in French. Subsequently, during a stop on the trip, he searched the women's cars, asking for the girl who spoke French. Finding her, he allowed Anna and several others to make several trips with a bucket to fetch water from a well. Before the last trip, Anna recalled: "He said, 'Listen to what I'm going to tell you, the three of you, just run away. I'm going to pretend I don't see you, I'll shoot later. Just go.'" Anna continued, "I didn't trust him, and we came back. Lots of times the Germans played games; I thought he'd shoot us. Then he appeared again, bringing us food, and then he told me, said 'I'm sorry, I gave you a chance to run away, I'm sorry that you didn't take a chance, because where you are going, you're not coming back.' He had a bottle of liquor he gave to me, with name (Leo Bernard) and address (on the French border), 'if you ever run away I'll help you.'" Years later she wrote Bernard, but the letter came back undelivered.[71]

In the open men's cars at the end of the train, the trip was made without food or water but also without fatalities. Though the open cars had boards laid over the top, on which a guard stood, and the prisoners had to sit the entire trip as a measure to prevent escape attempts, they were very aware of how "lucky" they were in comparison to the men in the closed cars.[72] In the closed cars the heat and suffocating lack of air dominated a struggle to survive. Nineteen-year-old Ruben Z. was "very lucky" to find a place beside the small window for fresh air at the beginning of the trip. He got several beatings from people who were desperate to get near the window, and he was finally pushed away and lost his place. He became so dizzy and weak that he could not remember what happened thereafter, other than that fifteen people had died in his car by the time they reached Birkenau.[73] Maurice W. remembers protesting to Becker as he was being driven into a car overfilled with 120 to 150 men. Becker kicked him and threatened to shoot him for his "impudence." In his car twenty-seven men suffocated during the trip.[74] Henry A. estimated that 150 prisoners had been packed into his car and that three passed out and were dead when they arrived.[75] Josef K. estimated that 120 men were loaded into his car. In the unbelievable heat, without food or water, men struggled to get near the window. "To me it seemed like a madhouse. Everything seemed to get wild. Bitter fights broke out over nothing. Were we in hell? Here the dying, there the unconscious, the screamers, those flailing wildly about. . . . It was a huge relief for us, when we finally arrived in Birkenau, the gassing camp of Auschwitz. Better already dead than to perish in such a death house. In our car out of 120 men 30 were dead."[76]

Among the dead when the train arrived in Birkenau were the head of the camp council, Jeremiah Wilczek, and his younger son, as well as Rubenstein, the man whom Wilczek had appointed head of the camp kitchen, and a number of other "Prominenten" of the Wilczek clique. Had they, like so many others, perished from dehydration, heat prostration, and suffocation? Or did their deaths signify something more sinister? In the very earliest testimony of August 1945, Mendel K., when complaining that the camp elite had enriched itself at the prisoners' expense, noted cryptically, "Later they were punished with the death they deserved." He promised to return to the matter. However, his account ends abruptly with the daylight breakout attempts on the day before the evacuation, and a fuller explanation is never given.[77] None of the other early testimonies even mention Wilczek's death, much less the circumstances surrounding it.

In the mid-1960s, when German investigators began interviewing survivors to assemble evidence against Becker, several witnesses explained Wilczek's death as yet another matter for which Becker should be held legally responsible. Matys F. told the investigators that Becker had conducted the loading of the train and especially sought out the "prominent Jews" and put them in a closed car packed with 120 prisoners. Matys F.'s own car was not nearly as crowded, and there had been open cars as well, in which no one suffocated. Thus the eighteen "Prominenten" who died on the way to Auschwitz had been, in effect, killed by Becker.[78] Hersz T. likewise accused Becker of crowding twice as many men into the closed as opposed to the open cars, "above all, the camp elders, camp leader, and camp police," in which many (allegedly 90 percent—a vast exaggeration) died from the heat.[79]

At the same time the investigators also heard a different version of events. Dina T., the daughter of the Starachowice rabbi, remembered that a man named Rubenstein as well as the head of the camp police, Wilczek, had been killed in a train car in route to Auschwitz.[80] And Ruth W., noting the large number of dead in the train cars upon arrival in Auschwitz, added that "in the men's cars, in any case, some prisoners were said to have killed others; for example, especially members of the camp administration were said to have been killed."[81] And Mayer G., who had escaped in the nighttime breakout, confirmed that he had heard after the war that a policeman and his son had been killed by other prisoners.[82]

In subsequent interviews, survivors were obviously reluctant to confirm in front of German investigators a story that both shifted blame for at least some Jewish deaths from the Germans to fellow Jews in general and acquitted Becker of responsibility in particular. Only one further witness stated outright that Wilczek and Rubenstein had been strangled in the train car on the way to Auschwitz.[83] Another specifically signaled out Becker for blame. "At the loading for Auschwitz Becker sought out people whom he knew particularly well, for example, people who had given him gifts, members of the Jewish council or people who had had special functions in the camp. He had them locked in a closed car pressed together as tightly together as possible. On the trip to Auschwitz many died. Among them were the camp policeman Jarmia Wilczek and his son."[84] But most were vague. Some merely confirmed that Wilczek and Rubenstein had died on the trip, without specifying how.[85] Others referred to altercations and trampling in the overcrowded car carrying the camp "Prominenten" and remarked that many did not arrive alive in Auschwitz.[86] Two witnesses conceded that the camp leaders had all been crowded into one car, in which prisoners had killed one another.[87] But all of these testimonies were hearsay. The German investigators stopped pursuing the issue entirely, when they heard from one witness, Ben L., who had actually ridden in the first car. "We were between 104 and 120 men locked in a sealed cattle car and received neither food nor water during the journey. Because it was the height of the summer of 1944, it was very hot, and the air holes in the car were too small to supply enough air for so many people. . . . In our car there were twenty dead upon arrival in Auschwitz. But it is not true, and this I want to declare emphatically, that the men had killed one another. I would say that most died from lack of air."[88]

Ben L.'s 1967 emphatic denial notwithstanding, in 1991 two survivors independently gave accounts that lifted the veil on the fate of Wilczek and other camp leaders on the train to Auschwitz. In a barely audible and technically flawed videotaped testimony that would nonetheless become part of the Fortunoff Archive collection, one survivor was explaining the tensions and conflict that arose between the camp council controlled by Wilczek and the Starachowice old timers on the one hand and the newly arrived young men from Majdanek, the so-called Lubliners or KLs, on the other. In conclusion, she noted, almost as an aside, that the Lubliners then killed twenty of the camp elite on the train to Auschwitz. Perhaps taken aback by the realization that she had said something she had not intended, she paused and then said with resignation that that, too, was also a part of history. In a retaping of her interview eighteen months later, she did not repeat the story.[89]

In the same year, 1991, Goldie Szachter Kalib published her memoir, *The Last Selection: A Child's Journey through the Holocaust.* Through contact with his boyhood friend, Shlomo Enesman of the Starachowice Judenrat and later of the camp council, her father had been able to obtain work papers for his family before the ghetto liquidation, and the immediate family had survived Strelnica and Majowka intact. She related how, immediately upon arrival in Auschwitz, she learned of the death of her father and brother, who had ridden in the ill-fated first car. A male friend of her sister "sadly explained that when the Judenrat stepped into the train at Starachowice, the KL Sonderkommando who had arrived in Starachowice from the Majdanek Concentration Camp aggressively forced its way into the same car. . . . The heat and lack of circulation in the closely packed car brought people close to suffocation. As some of the former Judenrat members were attempting to maneuver themselves into a less awkward standing position, individuals of the KL Sonderkommando began taunting: 'Who do you think you're pushing around? What makes you thing you're better than anyone else?' Tempers began to flare on both sides until the KL Sonderkommando thundered, 'All you pigs refused to share your privileges with anyone except those who were willing and able to make you rich. We'll show you what big shots you are now.' And fighting broke out. Father desperately attempted to calm the violence, only to incur the wrath of the KL Sonderkommando, who now turned on him." As her brother moved to defend her father, the "ruffians" began assaulting him too. The fight resulted in a number of fatalities, including her forty-four-year-old father and sixteen-year-old brother.[90]

Subsequently, eight Starachowice survivors giving videotaped testimony mentioned killing on the train to Auschwitz, five of them specifically identifying the victims as members of the Jewish council or police.[91] The fate of the Wilczek coterie and others at the hands of the Lubliners was also confirmed in six personal interviews.[92] For almost all of them, it was a matter of relating what they had learned from others immediately upon arrival in Auschwitz. The bodies of the dead were in plain sight as the Starachowice Jews disembarked and marched past the first car. And the sensational news of how the deaths had occurred traveled very fast. But one of those I interviewed was himself in the first car and could confirm the events as a direct eyewitness. As the Jews were being loaded onto the train in Starachowice, Henry G. spotted the Lubliners. "I looked at these guys who had just arrived to our camp. They were pretty strong yet. They came from another place, another camp. I said why don't I run with these guys, they look toughened up. . . . Maybe they'll escape; I'll run with them. They stuck us in that wagon and sealed us up. Strong guys, pretty good-sized boys." Wilczek, Rubenstein, and others of the camp elite were also in the car. "They stuck us in there like sardines. That's when the commotion started, fighting during the day, everybody tried to get a little bit of fresh air through that little window, they were pushing one another, getting angry." And then the killing began. Henry G. arrived in Birkenau sitting on the pile of corpses.

As a general rule, historians tend to prefer testimony that is given closer to the event in question to that given much later. But what is valid as a general rule is clearly not valid in the case of the fate of Jeremiah Wilczek and other camp leaders. Some events require a passage of time and the appropriate setting before witnesses are willing to speak. Clearly, the German investigation of Becker in the 1960s was not the propitious occasion and the German judicial investigators were not the suitable interviewers for Holocaust survivors to discuss this painful episode of internecine strife and revenge killing of Jews by Jews. By the 1990s, some fifty years after the fateful train ride to Birkenau, many of the Starachowice survivors were willing to speak of these events not only among themselves as a private memory but now also to others as a public memory. In doing so, they have disproved yet another disparaging cliché about Holocaust survivor testimony that as time passes it becomes more simplified and sanitized and divorced from the perplexing ambiguities and terrifying complexities of an increasingly distant time and place. Some still speak with anger and others with resignation, but they have spoken. The only voice that has not been heard is that of the Lubliners themselves. They apparently have not kept up any contact with the other Starachowice survivors, and not a single one of them is in my collection of 173 survivor witnesses. The gulf that separated them from the other prisoners in the camp and culminated in the train-car killings apparently has never been bridged.

I have argued that overall the core of shared memory of the Starachowice survivors has proved relatively stable and reliable, despite the fact that the testimonies were given in a time span stretching over fifty-six years. And as we have seen in the case of the fate of Wilczek, there has not been a growing tendency for increased silence about sensitive or taboo topics as time passes. Unfortunately, in partial contradiction to these generalizations I have just made, a chronological treatment of our topic requires me to end with precisely that episode—the arrival in Birkenau—about which survivor memory has proved increasingly problematic with the passage of time. In this case, however, another extremely important and complicating factor is at work.

The factory slave labor camp is one of the most understudied and least well known phenomena of the Holocaust, and among such camps, Starachowice was both small and obscure. Except for those who were enslaved there, it is virtually unknown. For the historian, this has the significant advantage that survivor memories of Starachowice are relatively pristine and uncontaminated by the later incorporation into individual memories of archetypal images broadly disseminated in popular consciousness. The arrival in Birkenau, on the other hand, is an extraordinarily dramatic, archetypal Holocaust memory, graphically described in some of the most widely read memoirs, such as Wiesel's *Night* and Levi's *Survival in Auschwitz* and visually portrayed in numerous documentaries and movies, most famously of course *Schindler's List*. How have the Starachowice survivors withstood the tendency to incorporate into their own memories the powerful and pervasive images about the arrival in Birkenau to which they have been exposed at a later date?

On one important count, the clear preponderance of testimony is quite convincing that the entry of the Starachowice transport into Birkenau was untypical. Because the transport came from a work camp that had already undergone numerous selections, the Starachowice prisoners were brought into Auschwitz as a group without being subjected to the notorious selection on the ramp. Particularly those who were children or still had children in their family at the time were emphatic on this point. The unusual admission into Birkenau without selection was perhaps the single most crucial stroke of luck or act of fate in a long chain of fortuitous and unlikely events that enabled them to survive.[93] In the words of one survivor, they were "the luckiest transport."[94] Another survivor simply concluded that the Germans were not going to fire up the crematoria for a few kids.[95] But for many, a more "miraculous" explanation was needed, and hence the story spread that Baumgarten had intervened on behalf of his former prisoners and sent a letter with the transport assuring the authorities in Birkenau that the Starachowice Jews were all good workers.[96] This explanation took its most extreme form in the testimonies of two survivors, one of which claimed that Baumgarten turned out after the war to have been a British secret agent and the other that he was really a Jew who had successfully concealed his identity.[97]

More common than the elaboration of an explanation as to why no selection had taken place was the memory that the transport had indeed undergone selection. Eleven survivors testified to this effect. All of these testimonies date from 1980 and later. Perhaps not surprisingly, ten survivors remember encountering the notorious Dr. Mengele on the ramp that morning of arrival as well.[98] In one survivor testimony, a selection occurred not on the ramp but after the showers, and it was conducted not by Mengele but rather by the equally infamous Adolf Eichmann.[99]

In my judgment, at least two factors are at work here. First, as mentioned above, the selection on the ramp by Dr. Mengele has become one of the most broadly recognized archetypal episodes of the Holocaust, widely disseminated in both books and films. Second, all of the Starachowice prisoners who arrived in Birkenau were later subjected to the routine selections of the camp conducted by SS doctors, and Mengele not infrequently took part in those. Thus both ex post facto incorporation of widely disseminated images as well as the telescoping of the subsequent experience of selection by SS doctors, including the notorious and feared Dr. Mengele, with the arrival in Birkenau, experienced in a state of utter exhaustion and trauma, could both contribute to the vivid memory of something that actually had not occurred. Under the circumstances, I would suggest that it is both surprising and ultimately an affirmation of the stability of the core memory of Starachowice survivors that a clear preponderance of testimony still points to the atypical nature of their arrival in Birkenau.

The powerful capacity of popular media, especially film, to implant images and to shape the way in which stories are retold can be seen in yet another aspect of the Starachowice testimonies. Before 1990, only one testimony—that of Josef K. from 1948—told how upon arrival in Birkenau the Starachowice prisoners did not dare to hope until water rather than gas came from the showerheads.[100] This must have been a not uncommon experience, yet it does not again appear in the testimonies for nearly fifty years. Then, after the memorable shower scene in *Schindler's List,* no fewer than six testimonies include in their narrative a reference to that specific moment when water rather than gas came from the showerheads.[101] I might add that all six are videotaped testimonies of the Visual History Foundation founded by Steven Spielberg.

Despite the various difficulties in using survivor testimony as a historical source that we have encountered, I still must conclude by reaffirming the overall value of survivor testimony for writing Holocaust history in general and the history of the Starachowice camps in particular. Crucial to this historical enterprise, however, is critical analysis. Survivor testimony cannot be accorded a privileged status, immune from the same careful examination of evidence to which our profession routinely subjects other sources. This is troublesome to some, who consider it presumptuous that someone like myself, born safely in America in 1944 and enjoying a comfortable academic career, should sit "in judgment" on the memories and stories of those who were there. But the alternative is to consign survivor testimony to the realm of commemoration rather than history and to refrain from filling in gaps in our historical knowledge of the Holocaust that a careful use of survivor testimonies would otherwise permit us to do.

I would close with two further thoughts. First, despite all the systemic pressures of what Primo Levi referred to as the "law of the Lager" that mandated egotistical self-assertion at the cost of all human solidarity, the Starachowice camps were not characterized by total social atomization. Bonding was in fact quite common. In part it was a response to the dominant position held by the privileged Wilczek clique. Excluded from the elite, others formed their own groups, based on town of origin or camp from which they had come. But above all, the ties of immediate family held firm, and it is the collective fate of the family that is the main theme of many survivor testimonies.

Second, my history of the Starachowice camps, based on 173 survivor testimonies, is in many ways a story of untypical survival during the Holocaust. But in one regard it is not at all untypical, namely, that it is not a particularly edifying story. One of the saddest "lessons" of the Holocaust is confirmation that terrible persecution does not ennoble victims. A few magnificent exceptions notwithstanding, persecution, enslavement, starvation, and mass murder do not make ordinary people into saints and heroic martyrs. The suffering of the victims, both those who survived and those who did not, is the overwhelming reality. We must be grateful for the testimonies of those who survived and are willing to speak, but we have no right to expect from them tales of edification and redemption.

Notes

Abbreviations

All.Proz.	Allgemeine Prozesse
BA Koblenz	Bundesarchiv Koblenz
Becker	Investigation of Walter Becker, Hamburg StA 147 Js 1312/63, 206 AR Z 39/62, Zentralstelle der Landesjustizverwaltungen
DKHH	*Der Dienstkalendar Heinrich Himmlers 1941/42*, ed. by Peter Witte et al (Hamburg, 1999)
FA	Fortunoff Archives, Sterling Library, Yale University
MJH	Museum of Jewish Heritage
NA	National Archives, Washington, D.C.
PA	Politisches Archiv des Auswärtigen Amtes, Berlin
TAE	*The Trial of Adolf Eichmann: Record of the Proceedings in the District Court of Jerusalem* (Jerusalem, 1993)
UMD	University of Michigan–Dearborn, Voice/Vision Holocaust Survivor Oral History Archive
USHMM	United States Holocaust Memorial Museum, Washington, D.C.
VHF	Survivors of the Shoah Visual History Foundation, Los Angeles
ZStL	Zentralstelle der Landesjustizverwaltungen, Ludwigsburg

Chapter 1. Perpetrator Testimony

1. Hannah Arendt, *Eichmann in Jerusalem: A Report on the Banality of Evil*, rev. and enl. ed. (New York, 1965), pp. 54, 252.

2. Yaacov Lozowick, *Hitler's Bureaucrats: The Nazi Security Police and the Banality of Evil* (New York, 2002), pp. 277–79.

3. Robert-Jan van Pelt, "A Site in Search of a Mission," in *Anatomy of the Auschwitz Death Camp* (Bloomington, 1994), ed. Yisrael Gutman and Michael Berenbaum, pp. 93–156.

4. For the most penetrating analysis of the Höss testimony, see Karin Orth, "Rudolf Höss und die 'Endlösung der Judenfrage,'" *Werkstattgeschichte* 18 (1997): 45–57.

5. The most thorough inventories of Eichmann's testimonies are found in Christian Gerlach, "The Eichmann Interrogations in Holocaust Historiography," *Holocaust and Genocide Studies* 15, no. 3 (winter 2001): 430–31, and Irmtrud Wojak, *Eichmanns Memoiren: Ein Kritischer Essay* (Frankfurt, 2001).

6. File 17 is available in *The Trial of Adolf Eichmann: Record of the Proceedings in the District Court of Jerusalem* (hereafter TAE), vol. 9 (Jerusalem: Trust for the Publication of the Proceedings of the Eichmann Trial, in cooperation with the Israel State Archives and Yad Vashem, 1992–95), microfiche copy of trial exhibit T-1393. In my opinion file 17 is the most notoriously unreliable and transparently mendacious of Eichmann's accounts. His calculations minimizing the numbers of Jews killed are absurd and border on Holocaust denial.

7. Wojak, *Eichmanns Memoiren*, pp. 24, 48, 50, 217–18.

8. "Eichmann Tells His Own Damning Story," *Life*, 28 November and 5 December 1960. Staff writers from *Life* claimed that they were able to read through the entire transcripts and make their own selections, in their own view including the self-incriminating material but, insofar as possible, leaving out the self-justifications. Edward Thompson, Managing Editor, to Raul Hilberg, 1 December 1960. I am grateful to Raul Hilberg for providing me a copy of this letter from his private correspondence.

9. Wojak, *Eichmanns Memoiren*, p. 52, confirms that *Ich, Adolf Eichmann* was based on the Sassen tapes and not on separate notes written in the early 1950s, as the publisher's foreword alleges.

10. *Ich, Adolf Eichmann: Ein historischer Zeugenbericht*, ed. Dr. Rudolf Aschenauer (Leoni Am Starnberger See, 1980), pp. 177–79.

11. On Sassen's agenda, see Wojak, *Eichmanns Memoiren*, pp. 49, 57, 90–91. Wojak notes that Eichmann was interested primarily in shaping his own historical image, not in whitewashing Hitler.

12. Wojak, *Eichmanns Memoiren*, pp. 57–58, 62–65, 80–81, 91.

13. Leni Yahil, who has compared portions of the Sassen transcripts in the Israeli State Archives with the Aschenauer volume, has come to the same conclusion concerning his tendentious distortions. See her "'Memoirs' of Adolf Eichmann," *Yad Vashem Studies* 18 (1987): 133–62.

14. Wojak, *Eichmanns Memoiren*, p. 50, confirms that the occasional pop from the uncorking of wine bottles can be heard on the tapes.

15. TAE, vol. 4, pp. 1600, 1606, 1619–20, 1664–65, 1759–62, 1796–97, 1822–23.

16. TAE, vols. 7–8.

17. Photostat copies are in the Yad Vashem Archives and the Zentralstelle der Landesjustizverwaltungen in Ludwigsburg. I am endebted to Michael Waldbaum, a volunteer at Yad Vashem, who deciphered the handwriting and helped me construct a typescript of this document in Jerusalem in 1981.

18. For example, Christopher R. Browning, *Fateful Months: Essays on the Emergence of the Final Solution* (New York, 1985), pp. 23–24.

19. Allgemeine Prozesse (hereafter All. Proz.) 6/169, Bundesarchiv Koblenz (hereafter BA Koblenz). For Eichmann's comments on the origins of these timelines in his court testimony, see TAE, vol. 4, pp. 1833–34.

20. TAE, vol. 4.

21. Eichmann post-trial memoirs "Götzen," Israel State Archives. Christian Gerlach, "The Eichmann Interrogations in Holocaust Historiography," p. 442, in particular has pointed out the grotesque nature of "Eichmann-the-Colleague."

22. TAE, vol. 4, pp. 1375, 1802, 1827–28; vol. 7, pp. 89, 113–15; "Götzen," part 1, pp. 21–28.

23. TAE, vol. 4, pp. 1591, 1829.

24. TAE, vol. 4, pp. 1376–78, 1399; vol. 7, pp. 83, 101–7, 134, 1380–89; vol. 8, pp. 2501, 2527; "Meine Memoiren," pp. 63–75; "Götzen," part 1, pp. 65–70, 74–77.

25. Wojak, *Eichmanns Memoiren*, p. 99.

26. TAE, vol. 4, pp. 1593, 1602–4; vol. 7, pp. 121–25; "Meine Memoiren," pp. 80–83; "Götzen," part 1, pp. 111–13.

27. TAE, vol. 4, pp. 1396, 1609, 1616; vol. 7, p. 137; vol. 8, p. 2478; "Meine Memoiren," pp. 88–92; "Götzen," part 1, p. 143a.

28. TAE, vol. 7, pp. 116–18, 135–36; "Meine Memoiren," pp. 76–79; "Götzen," part 1, pp. 84–89.

29. TAE, vol. 7, pp. 126, 140, 149; "Götzen," part 1, p. 112.

30. TAE, vol. 4, p. 1568.

31. TAE, vol. 4, pp. 1397, 1406, 1418, 1424, 1568, 1661–62, 1698–99, 1830–31; vol. 7, 196, 203, 490–91, 673; "Götzen," part 1, p. 106. On the Sassen tapes, Eichmann had proclaimed: "I was not a normal recipient of orders, because that would have made me an idiot; I thought about things as well, I was an idealist." TAE, vol. 4, p. 1791.

32. For example: Rauff's memo noting Eichmann's presence at Heydrich's meeting of 21 September 1939, Rademacher's marginal note of 13 September 1941 that Eichmann had proposed shooting the Serbian Jews, and Wetzel's 25 October 1941 draft mentioning a discussion with Eichmann over constructing a gas van in Riga. Wojak, *Eichmanns Memoiren*, pp. 105, 174.

33. Gerlach, "The Eichmann Interrogations in Holocaust Historiography," pp. 429, 434, 442.

34. Zeitplan 1942, All. Proz. 6/169, BA Koblenz .

35. "Meine Memoiren," pp. 110–11.

36. Zeitpläne 1941 and 1942, All. Proz. 6/169, BA Koblenz.

37. TAE, vol. 4, p. 1705.

38. *Der Dienstkalendar Heinrich Himmlers 1941/42* (hereafter DKHH), ed. Peter Witte et al. (Hamburg, 1999), p. 513.

39. TAE, vol. 7, pp. 229–30. When telling Less of this visit, he temporarily confused the Treblinka site with his first visit to a camp under construction in the Lublin district and mentions seeing the same wood house on the right and two to three wood houses on the left. He makes clear, however, that the gas chamber was not one of these houses but a larger hall-like building.

40. TAE, vol. 4, p. 1762.

41. TAE, vol. 7, pp. 218, 372–76.

42. TAE, vol. 7, pp. 380, 383, 394.

43. Zeitplan 1942, All. Proz. 6/169, BA Koblenz.

44. "Götzen," p. 166.

45. Sybille Steinbacher, *"Musterstadt" Auschwitz. Germanisierungspolitik und Judenmord in Ostoberschlesien* (Munich, 2000), p. 286. For the East Upper Silesia transports, see also BD 23/5 (International Tracing Service Arolsen),Yad Vashem Archives, Jerusalem (hereafter YVA), and RG 15.030M, microfiche 1, Nachvezeichnis aller aus Beuthen O/S ausgesiedelten Juden, United States Holocaust Memorial Museum (hereafter USHMM).

46. Deborah Dwork and Robert-Jan van Pelt, *Auschwitz: 1270 to the Present* (New York, 1996), p. 305.

47. Rudolf Höss, *Commandant of Auschwitz* (New York, Popular Library Edition, 1951), p. 141.

48. "Eichmann Tells His Own Damning Story," *Life*, 28 November 1960.

49. *Ich, Adolf Eichmann,* pp. 180–81.

50. TAE, vol. 7, 239–40, 846.

51. "Meine Memoiren," pp. 116–17.

52. Zeitplan 1942, All. Proz. 6/169, BA Koblenz.

53. TAE, vol. 4, pp. 1710–11.

54. According to Wojak, *Eichmanns Memoiren*, p. 176, at one point in the Sassen interviews Eichmann gave the date as "fall 1941."

55. "Eichmann Tells His Own Damning Story," *Life*. When shown the *Life* article, Eichmann made corrections. He wrote that he had not seen "busses" but rather only one "bus," and that it was entirely enclosed without windows. He also denied riding on the bus and said he followed the bus in a car. TAE, vol. 9, trial exhibit T/48 (microfiche).

56. TAE, vol. 7, pp. 174–77.

57. "Meine Memoiren," pp. 105–7.

58. Zeitplan 1941, All. Proz. 6/169, BA Koblenz.

59. TAE, vol. 4, pp. 1560, 1672.

60. "Götzen," pp. 126–28.

61. "Eichmann Tells His Own Damning Story," *Life*.

62. TAE, vol. 7, pp. 210–15; vol. 8, 2485–86.

63. "Meine Memoiren," p. 109.

64. Zeitplan 1942, All. Proz. 6/169, BA Koblenz.

65. TAE, vol. 4, p. 1560–61.

66. "Götzen," pp. 135–37.

67. Peter Witte editorial comment to the Eichmann text, *Die Welt,* 31 August 1999. Wojak, *Eichmanns Memoiren*, p. 172, assumes the fall 1941 dating of the trip to Lwow but does not note Eichmann's alternative dating to the summer of 1942.

68. Christian Gerlach, *Kalkulierte Morde: Die deutsche Wirtschafts- und Vernichtungspolitik in Weissrussland 1941 bis 1944* (Hamburg, 1999), pp. 693–94. Likewise, in "The Eichmann Interrogations in Holocaust Historiography," p. 436, Gerlach says this Minsk trip can be dated "almost certainly" to 2–3 March 1942.

69. Dannecker memo, 10 March 1942, printed in Serge Klarsfeld, *Vichy-Auschwitz: Die Zusammenarbeit der deutschen und französischen Behörden bei der Endlösung der Judenfrage in Frankreich* (Nördlingen, 1983), p. 374.

70. On March 6 Eichmann chaired a meeting of representatives

from the Stapoleitstellen to orient them to the next wave of deportations. Simultaneously, other experts were meeting in the same building to discuss the status of Mischlinge and mixed marriage, two issues unresolved at the Wannsee Conference.

71. My interpretation of the timing and function of Eichmann's trip to Minsk is in full accord with that of Irmtrud Wojak. *Eichmanns Memoiren,* pp. 171–72.

72. TAE, vol. 7, pp. 165; "Meine Memoiren," p. 104.

73. "Eichmann Tells His Own Damning Story," *Life.*

74. *Ich, Adolf Eichmann,* pp. 178–79. Imtrud Wojak gives a verbatim quote from the Sassen tapes concerning Eichmann's hearing of the Füiherbefehl for the physical destruction of the Jews that is essentially the same, although considerably more garbled. *Eichmanns Memoiren,* pp. 181–82.

75. The phrase "turn of the year 1941/42" is from Eichmann's notoriously unreliable and exculpatory file 17, which also omits all mention of his key activities at this time, namely the visits to Lublin, Minsk, and Chelmno.

76. TAE, vol. 7, pp. 169–74.

77. TAE, vol. 7, pp. 372–74, 400.

78. "Meine Memoiren," pp. 94–98.

79. Zeitplan 1941, All. Proz. 6/169, BA Koblenz.

80. TAE, vol. 4, pp. 1559–60.

81. TAE, vol. 4, pp. 1416, 1673–74.

82. "Götzen," pp. 118–22.

83. "Götzen," pp. 144–45.

84. Peter Witte, "Auf Befehl des 'Führers,'" *Die Welt,* 27 August 1999. Christian Gerlach, "Die Wannsee-Konferenz, das Schicksal der deutschen Juden und Hitlers politische Grundsatzentscheidung, alle Juden Europas zu ermordern," *Werkstattgeschichte* 18 (1997): 31, and "The Eichmann Interrogations in Holocaust Historiography," p. 434; Wojak, *Eichmanns Memoiren,* pp. 183–84; discussions with Christian Gerlach and Hans Safrian. For Oberhauser testimony, see 8 AR-Z 252/9, IX, p. 1680 (Oberhauser testimony, 12 December 1962), Zentralstelle der Landesjustizverwaltungen (hereafter ZStL). For Polish witnesses, see 8 AR-Z 252/9, VI, pp. 1119–20 (Eustachy Urkainski testimony, 11 October 1945), and pp. 1129–32 (Stanislaw Kozak testimony, 14 October 1945), ZStL.

85. Affidavit of Hans Bodo Gorgass, 23 February 1947 (Nürnberg Document NO-3010), cited by Helmut Krausnick in *Der Mord an den*

Juden im zweiten Weltkrieg, ed. Eberhard Jäckel and Jürgen Rohwer (Stuttgart, 1985), pp. 139–40.

86. Wojak, *Eichmanns Memoiren,* p. 183, proposes early March 1942.

87. My own observations from visiting the site are shared by Michael Tregenza, "Belzec—Das vergessene Lager des Holocaust," in *"Arisierung" im Nationalsozialismus. Volksgemeinschaft, Raub und Gedächtnis,* ed. Irmtrud Wojak and Peter Hayes (Frankfurt and New York, 2000), p. 247.

88. Cited in Bogdan Musial, *Deutsche Zivilverwaltung und Judenverfolgung im Generalgouvernement,* pp. 205–6. Hahnzog dated this to the spring, not the fall, of 1941.

89. Bernhard Lösener, "Als Rassereferent," pp. 302–3. See *Die Tagebücher von Joseph Goebbels,* Teil II, Bd. 1, ed. Elke Fröhlich (Munich, 1996), pp. 265–66, 269, 278 (entries of 19 and 20 August 1941), for the Hitler-Goebbels discussions on the topic.

90. Höppner Aktenvermerk, 2 September 1941, and Höppner to Ehrlich and Eichmann, 3 September 1941, 8/103/45–62, RG 15.007m, USHMM. The Aktenvermerk is printed in *Vom Generalplan Ost zum Generalsiedlungsplan,* ed. Czeslaw Madajczyk (Munich, 1994), appendix 3, pp. 392–96.

91. Rademacher marginalia, 13 September 1941, on Benzler to AA, 12 September 1941, Inland IIg 194, Politisches Archiv des Auswärtigen Amtes (hereafter PA).

92. Peter Witte, "Two Decisions Concerning the 'Final Solution to the Jewish Question': Deportations to Lodz and Mass Murder in Chelmno," *Holocaust and Genocide Studies* 9, no. 3 (winter 1995): 327–28.

93. Himmler to Greiser, 18 September 1941, microfilm, T-175/54/ 2568695, National Archives, Washington, D.C. (hereafter NA). Hans Frank of the General Government rejected a plan to share the burden, refusing to accept even two trainloads of Hamburg Jews into the General Government. Türk to KHM Hrubieszow, 7 October 1941, O-53/ 85/1036, YVA. Himmler had clearly been working to find reception areas for Reich Jews weeks before this. On September 2, 1941, Himmler met with the Higher SS and Police Leader of the General Government, Friedrich Wilhelm Krüger, and discussed the "Jewish Question—Resettlement from the Reich." He then met with Krüger's counterpart from the Warthegau, Wilhelm Koppe, two days later, possibly to discuss the same topic. DKHH, pp. 200–203 and 205, especially footnote 19.

94. *Die Tagebücher von Joseph Goebbels,* Teil II, Bd. 2, pp. 480–82, 485 (entry of 24 September 1941).

95. I am extremely grateful to Dr. Charles Sydnor Jr. for his advice in reconstructing Reinhard Heydrich's itinerary between mid-September and late October.

96. Philippe Burrin, *Hitler and the Jews: The Genesis of the Final Solution* (London, 1994), p. 127.

97. 8 AR-Z 252/9, V, pp. 925–30 (testimony of Hans-Joachim B.), ZStL.

98. Danuta Czech, *Kalendarium der Ereignisse im Konzentrationslager Auschwitz-Birkenau 1939–1945* (Hamburg, 1989), pp. 115–19, 122.

99. Mathais Beer, "Die Entwicklung der Gaswagen beim Mord an den Juden," *Vierteljarhshefte für Zeitgeschichte* 35, no. 3 (1987): 407–8; Christian Gerlach, "Failure of Plans for an SS Extermination Camp in Mogilev, Belorussia," *Holocaust and Genocide Studies* 11, no. 1 (spring 1997): 65.

100. Again, I am grateful to Dr. Charles Sydnor Jr. for the Heydrich itinerary.

101. On this day Heydrich met with both officials of the Ostministerium (Nürnberg Document NO-1020: meeting of Heydrich, Meyer, Schlatterer, Leibbrandt, and Ehlich, 4 October 1941) and Undersecretary Luther of the Foreign Office. Christopher R. Browning, *The Final Solution and the German Foreign Office* (New York, 1978), p. 59.

102. Uebelhoer to Himmler, 9 October 1941, microfilm, T-175/54/2568653–4, NA. From the Uebelhoer letter, we learn that on September 29, Eichmann incorrectly reported in Berlin that the Lodz ghetto was being divided into sections for workers and nonworkers. On that same day Eichmann also wrote Höppner and informed him that "at the moment" *(zur Zeit)* there would be no resumption of the expulsion of Jews and Poles into the General Government but that he was looking for reception areas on occupied Soviet territory. Götz Aly, *"Endlösung": Völkerverschiebung und der Mord an den europäischen Juden* (Frankfurt, 1995), pp. 350–51.

103. *Die Tagebücher von Joseph Goebbels*, Teil II, Bd. 2, p. 84.

104. Notes on conference of 10 October 1941 in Prague, printed in H. G. Adler, *Theresienstadt, 1941–1945: Das Anlitz einer Zwangsgemeinschaft*, 2nd ed. (Tübingen, 1960), document 46b, pp. 720–22.

105. DKHH, pp. 233–35.

106. Hans Frank, *Das Diensttagebuch des deutschen Generalgouverneurs in Polen 1939–1945*, ed. Werner Präg and Wolfgang Jacobmeyer (Stuttgart, 1975), p. 413 (Aktennotiz of Frank-Rosenberg meeting, 13 October 1941).

107. The meeting was important enough that Globocnik reported to Himmler personally about it on October 25, 1941. DKHH, p. 246.

108. Cited in Musial, *Deutsche Zivilverwaltung und Judenverfolgung im Generalgouvernment*, pp. 196–98. Musial found these remarks in hitherto unpublished sections of the Frank Tagebuch.

109. *Diensttagebuch*, p. 436 (Regierungssitzung in Lwow, 21 October 1941).

110. Luther memoranda, 13 and 17 October 1941, Politische Abteilung III 245, PA.

111. DKHH, p. 238.

112. Rademacher report, 25 October 1941, *Akten zur deutschen auswärtigen Politik*, D, XIII, Part 2 (Göttingen, 1970), pp. 570–72.

113. Wurm to Rademcher, 23 October 1941, Inland A/B 59/3, PA.

114. Abromeit Vermerk, 24 October 1941, on meeting in Berlin on 23 October 1941, O-53/76/110–111, YVA.

115. V 203 AR-Z 69/59 (Urteil, Landgericht Bonn, 8 Ks 2/63, pp. 24 and 94); 203 AR-Z 69/59, IV, 624–43, and VI, 961–89 (testimony of Walter Burmeister), ZStL.

116. Gerlach, "Failure of Plans for an Extermination Center in Mogilev, Belorussia," *Holocaust and Genocide Studies* 11, no. 1 (spring 1997): 60–64; Gerlach, *Kalkulierte Morde*, pp. 650–53. Rolf Ogorreck, "Die Einsatzgruppen der Sicherheitspolizei und des Sicherheitsdienst im Rahme der 'Genesis der Endlösung'" (Ph.D. diss., Free University Berlin, 1992), pp. 280 and 289, for German trial testimony about Himmler's discussion of killing Jews with gas during this visit.

117. Nürnberg Document NO-365: draft letter, Rosenberg to Lohse, initialed by Wetzel, 25 October 1941, VI 420 AR-Z 1439/65 (Wetzel testimony, 20 September 1961), ZStL. The letter did not in fact have to be sent, since Lohse arrived in Berlin that very day. Like German officials in Lodz, he was determined to stop the deportations to Riga. He dropped his opposition when he learned that the unwanted Jews would be sent "further to the east." Leibbrandt to RK Ostland, 13 November 1941, JM 3435, YVA.

118. *Monologe im Führerhauptquartier, 1941–1944: Die Aufzeichnungen Heinrich Helms*, ed. Werner Jochmann (Hamburg, 1980), p. 106 (entry of 25 October 1941).

Chapter 2. Survivor Testimonies from Starachowice

1. Henry Greenspan, "The Awakening of Memory: Survivor Testimony in the First Years after the Holocaust, and Today," Monna and Otto Weinmann Annual Lecture, May 2000, printed as an occasional

paper of the U.S. Holocaust Memorial Museum, 2001, and *On Listening to Holocaust Survivors: Recounting and Life History* (Westport, Conn., 1998).

2. Kenneth Jacobson, *Embattled Selves: An Investigation into the Nature of Identity through Oral Histories of Holocaust Survivors* (New York, 1994).

3. Nanette Auerhahn and Dori Laub, "Holocaust Testimony," *Holocaust and Genocide Studies* 5, no. 4 (winter 1990): 447–62.

4. Martin Bergman and Milton Jucovy, *Generations of the Holocaust* (New York, 1983); Aaron Hass, *In the Shadow of the Holocaust* (Ithaca, N.Y., 1990), and *The Aftermath: Living with the Holocaust* (New York, 1995).

5. William Helmreich, *Against All Odds: Holocaust Survivors and the Successful Lives They Made in America* (New York, 1997).

6. Larry Langer, *Holocaust Testimonies: The Ruins of Memory* (New Haven, 1991).

7. Elie Wiesel is the exemplar of this approach.

8. Peter Black, "A Response to Some New Approaches to the History of the Holocaust," *The New England Journal of History* 59, no. 1 (fall 2000): 47–48.

9. Jan Gross, *Neighbors: The Destruction of the Jewish Community in Jedwabne, Poland* (Princeton, 2001), pp. 139–40.

10. For the dilemma of writing a history of events whose essential characteristic was the destruction of potential witnesses, see Carlo Ginzburg, "Just One Witness," in *Probing the Limits of Representation: Nazism and the Final Solution*, ed. Saul Friedländer (Cambridge, Mass., 1992), pp. 82–96.

11. Gross, *Neighbors*, pp. 25–26.

12. Conversation with Nechama Tec.

13. Greenspan, "The Awakening of Memory," p. 20.

14. Felicja Karay, *Death Comes in Yellow: Skarzysko-Kamienna Slave Labor Camp* (Amsterdam, 1996).

15. Hamburg StA 147 Js 1312/63, investigation of Walter Becker (hereafter Becker), pp. 405 (testimony of Fred B.), 866 (Anna W.), 206 AR-Z 39/62, ZStL.

16. Becker, pp. 1006 (Mendel M.), 1021 (Simcha G.).

17. For a general background on the use of Jewish labor in Poland, see chapter 3 of my *Nazi Policy, Jewish Workers, German Killers* (Cambridge, 2000); Dieter Pohl, "Die grossen Zwangsarbeitslager der SS- und Polizeiführer für Juden im Generalgouvernement 1942–1945," in *Die nationalsozialistische Konzentrationslager: Entwicklung und Struktur*, ed. Ulrich Herbert, Karin Orth, and Christoph Dieckmann (Göttingen,

1998), vol. 1, pp. 415–38; Donald Bloxham, "'Extermination through Work': Jewish Slave Labour under the Third Reich," *Educational Trust Research Papers* 1, no. 1 (1999–2000), and "Jewish Slave Labour in Relation to the 'Final Solution,'" in *Remembering for the Future: The Holocaust in the Age of Genocide,* ed. John Roth (Hampshire and New York, 2001), pp. 163–86.

18. Landgericht Hamburg, Urteil (50) 35/70 in der Strafsache gegen Walter Becker, p. 17, ZStL; Becker, p. 732 (Alan N.); M-49E/155 (Simcha M.), YVA.

19. Becker, pp. 1414, 1417 (Akiva R.); Goldie Szachter Kalib, *The Last Selection: A Child's Journey through the Holocaust* (Amherst, Mass., 1991), pp. 170, 180, 199.

20. Becker, pp. 675 (Meyer H.), 759 (Mina B.), 792 (Leib R.), 831 (Ben L.); PCN 17158 (Paul C.), PCN 19958 (Miriam M.), PCN 18549 (Saul M.), PCN 11572 (Joseph T.), PCN 23509 (Anita T.), PCN 600447 (Chaim W.), Survivors of the Shoah Visual History Foundation (hereafter VHF); RG-1383 (Pola F.), Museum of Jewish Heritage (hereafter MJH); personal interview, Anna W., 2001.

21. Among the numerous references to Althoff's hospital barrack massacres, see Becker, pp. 29 (Israel A.), 83 (Mendel M.), 407 (Fred B.), 435 (Toby W.), 631 (Mania B), 749 (Leonia F.), 791 (Leib R.), 896 (Anna B.); T-91 (Israel A.), Fortunoff Archives, Sterling Library, Yale University (hereafter FA); Kalib, *The Last Selection,* pp. 177–79.

22. Becker, pp. 83–84 (Mendel M.), 425 (Jack S.), 491 (Ralph C.), 505 (Max S.), 509 (Dina T.), 515 (Ruth W.), 732 (Alan N.), 859, 1239 (Eva Z.), 865 (Anna W.), 897 (Anna B.), 1388 (Pinchas H.); M-49E/155 (Simcha M.), YVA; personal interview, Alan N., 2001.

23. Becker, pp. 818 (Faye G., who named Schwertner as the factory spokesman), 828 (Ben L., according to whom it was Becker who made this announcement); personal interview, Joseph F., 2002 (who attributed the announcement to Baumgarten); PCN 641059 (Louis F., who identifies the speaker only as a "civilian" from the factory), VHF.

24. Becker, pp. 776 (Arnold F.), 1390 (Chaim H.).

25. Becker, p. 869 (Anna W.).

26. Becker, pp. 470 (Adam G.), 714 (Ida G.), 859 (Eva Z.), 1328 (Alan N.), 1364 (Rachiel P.), 1369 (Max R.); M-49/1172 (Mendel K.), YVA; PCN 640106 (Rachel P.), VHF; personal interview, Alan N.; Adam Rutkowski, "Hitlerischen Arbeitslager für den Juden im Distrikt Radom," *Biuletyn Żydowskiego Instytutu Historycznego* 17/18 (1956): 19.

27. This shooting was the focal point of a judicial investigation of Gerhard Kaschmieder. II 206 AR 513/68, ZStL.

28. Becker, pp. 736–37 (Toby W.), 796 (Abraham R.), 938 (Zvi Hersh F.), 956 (Israel E.), 961 (Sarah P.), 970 (Rachmiel Z.), 1053 (Pinchas H.); PCN 5829 (Irene H.), VHF; Kalib, *The Last Selection*, p. 129.

29. Becker, pp. 1090–91 (Leopold Rudolf Schwertner); SS-enlisted men file, Berlin Document Center microfilms, NA.

30. Becker, pp. 868 (Anna W.), 873–74 (Adrian W.); M-49/1172 (Mendel K.), YVA.

31. Becker, pp. 65 (Rywka G.), 84 (Mendel M.), 406 (Fred B.), 592 (Mina B.).

32. Becker, pp. 781–82 (Rosa H.), 779–800 (Avraham R.), 804 (Syma R.), 810–811 (Helen W.), 849 (Ruth R.), 887 (Frymeta M.), 904 (Morka M.), 996 (Nathan G.), 1266 (Morris Z.); RG-1165 (Guta W.), MJH; personal interview, Martin B., 2001. Another "decent" German was Bruno Pape, the head of the "small forge." Personal interview, Joseph F.

33. M-1E.2469 (Joseph K.), YVA; T-1682 (Mania K.), FA.

34. M-49/1172 (Mendel K.), YVA; Becker, pp. 800 (Avraham R.), 880–81, 1271 (Morris Z.); RG-50.030*250 (Guta W.), USHMM; personal interview, Martin B.

35. Kalib, *The Last Selection*, pp. 173–74, 207; PCN 635637 (Salek B.), PCN 620109 (Tovi P.), VHF; personal interview, Joseph F.

36. Kalib, *The Last Selection*, pp. 200–203; PCN 620109 (Tovi P.), VHF.

37. PCN 620109 (Tovi P.), VHF.

38. Becker, p. 1335 (Moshe P.); T-1884 (Regina N.), FA; PCN 635637 (Salek B.), PCN 620109 (Tovi P.), VHF; Kalib, *The Last Selection*, p. 174.

39. T-955 (Guta T.), FA; O-3/9394 (Ruben Z.), YVA; Becker, p. 652 (Mayer G.).

40. M-49/1172 (Mendel K.), O-3/9394 (Ruben Z.), YVA; Becker, pp. 652 (Mayer G.), 728 (Bella W.).

41. M-49/1172 (Mendel K.), YVA; Becker, pp. 654–65 (Mayer G.).

42. Becker, pp. 425 (Jack S.), 804 (Syma R.), 896 (Anna B.); PCN 633693 (Rachel A.), VHF; Kalib, *The Last Selection*, p. 179; personal interview, Alan N.

43. M-49/1172 (Mendel K.), YVA; PCN 635637 (Salek B.), VHF; personal interview, Alan N.

44. M-49/1172 (Mendel K.) for Wolanow, YVA; PCN 634090 (Toby K., who testifies that prisoners arriving from Tomaszow were also robbed of their possessions by the camp police), VHF; personal interview, Alan N., that the Lubliners were robbed on arrival as well.

45. M-49/1172 (Mendel K.), YVA; T-1884 (Regina N.), FA; Kalib, *The Last Selection*, pp. 209–10; Henry K., Voice/Vision Holocaust Survivor Oral History Archive, University of Michigan–Dearborn (hereafter UMD); personal interview, Howard C., 2001.

46. Personal interview, Anna W.

47. Personal interview, Joseph F.

48. T-955 (Guta T.), FA; PCN 635637 (Salek B.), PCN 17158 (Paul C.), PCN 641059 (Louis F.), VHF.

49. M-49E/1669 (Leon W.), M-49/1172 (Mendel K.), YVA; Kalib, *The Last Selection*, pp. 171–72.

50. Becker, p. 492 (Ralph C.); M-49/1172 (Mendel K.), YVA; T-955 (Gutta T.), T-1884 (Regina N.), FA; PCN 17158 (Paul C.), VHF; personal interview, Alan N.; Kalib, *The Last Selection*, p. 176.

51. T-955 (Gutta T.), FA; O-3/9394 (Ruben Z.), YVA; Kalib, *The Last Selection*, pp. 172, 174, 180–81, 206, 208; PCN 635867 (Morris P.), VHF; RG-50.030*0396 (Chris L.), USHMM; personal interviews, Martin B., Howard C., Alan N.

52. Personal interview, Chris L.

Chapter 3. Survivor Testimonies from Starachowice

1. Becker, p. 772 (Arnold F., 1966). Survivors remember the date of the move differently. Arnold F. placed the move just weeks before the evacuation, that is, in early July. Alan N. dated it to April or May 1944. Becker, p. 735 (Alan N., 1967). Rachmiel Z. placed it in May. Becker, p. 101 (Rachmiel Z., 1962). Zvi Hersz U. placed it in the spring. Becker, p. 95 (Zvi Hersz U., 1962). Pinchas H. placed it in June. Becker, p. 79 (Pinchas H., 1962).

2. Personal interview, Howard C., 2001.

3. M-49/1172 (Mendel K., 1945), YVA.

4. M-1/E.2469 (Josef K., 1948), YVA; T-1682 (Mania K., 1988), FA; RG-1165 (Guta B. W., 1984), MJH; personal interview, Martin B., 2001.

5. M-49/1172 (Mendel K., 1945), YVA.

6. Donald Niewyk, who worked through all of the Boder testimonies and published edited versions of some of them, concluded that

Kalman E. "sought to dramatize his story to the hilt" and that "parts may strain credulity." Donald Niewyk, *Fresh Wounds: Early Narratives of Holocaust Survival* (Chapel Hill, 1998), p. 87.

7. David Boder Interviews (Kalman E., 1946), USHMM, portions printed in Niewyk, *Fresh Wounds*, pp. 87–93. The text of this interview can also be found on the Illinois Institute of Technology Web site.

8. M-1/E.2469 (Josef K., 1948), YVA.

9. Becker, p. 709 (Lea G., 1966).

10. Becker, p. 850 (Ruth R., 1967).

11. Becker, p. 782 (Rosa H., 1967).

12. RG-1383 (Pola F., 1986), MJH.

13. T-1682 (Mania K., 1988), FA.

14. Personal interview with Martin B., 2001. Though not a direct witness, Goldie Szachter Kalib related a somewhat different version of the incident, based on what she must have heard later. In her memoirs published in 1991, she wrote that when the trucks were about to leave the lumberyard, a young Jewish girl slapped a German officer in the face twice, and he merely walked away. *The Last Selection*, pp. 211–12.

15. Becker, pp. 1309–15 (Guta B. W., 1968). The protocol referred to an earlier interview in which Guta B. W. may have related her general story, but the protocol of this earlier interview unfortunately is not in the case records.

16. RG-1165 (Guta B. W., 1984), MJH; RG 50.030*250 (Guta B. W., 1990), USHMM.

17. Danuta Czech, *Kalendarium der Ereignisse im Konzentrationslager Auschwitz-Birkenau 1939–1945*, p. 832. This is also the precise date given by Goldie Szachter Kalib, *The Last Selection*, p. 218.

18. PCN 204998 (Leon M., 1996), VHF.

19. For testimony that explicitly placed the loading and unloading before the ensuing breakout: Becker, pp. 79–80 (Pinchas H., 1962), 95 (Zvi U., 1962); RG-1383 (Pola F., 1986), MJH. For those who explicitly placed the first breakout attempt before the loading and unloading: personal interview, Alan N., February 8, 2001; O 2/319 (Moses W., n.d.), YVA. In one account the train was loaded, unloaded, then reloaded in the same day: M-1/E.2469 (Josef K., 1948), YVA. Other accounts of the loading and unloading: Becker, pp. 518 (Ruth W., 1966), 787 (Max N., 1967), 805 (Symcha R., 1967), 816 (Alter W., 1967), 819 (Faye G., 1967), 826 (Ben Z., 1967), 1380 (Toby S., 1968), 1416 (Akiva R., 1968); personal interviews, Martin B. and Howard C., 2001.

20. PCN 620109 (Tova P., 1998), VHF.

21. RG-50.030*0396 (Chris L., 1998), USHMM.

22. M-49/1172 (Mendel K., 1945), YVA.

23. Becker, pp. 372 (Moshe R., 1966), 414 (Anna A., 1966). Two others mention only that Herblum was subsequently held responsible. Becker, pp. 1369 (Max R., 1968), 1397 (Salamon B., 1968).

24. T-91 (Israel A., 1980), FA.

25. Personal interview, Regina N., 2001; T-1884 (Regina N., 1991 and 1992), FA.

26. PCN 629188 (Esther K., 1997), VHF.

27. Becker, pp. 826 (Ben Z., 1967), 856 (Israel C., 1967); PCN 5829 (Irene H., 1995), VHF.

28. PCN 14818 (Joseph Z., 1995), VHF.

29. PCN 11572 (Joseph T., 1997), VHF.

30. Israel A., Toby Wo., Ralph C., Toby We., Alan N., Jankiel C., Regina N., Lena W., Pola F., Henry G., Emil N., Mendel K., Leonia F., Kalman E., Louis F.

31. PCN 641059 (Louis F., 1998), VHF; Becker, p. 23 (Mach A., 1962).

32. For the payment, RG-1984 (Regina N., 1988), MJH; T-1884 (Regina N., 1991 and 1992), FA; personal interview, Regina N., 2001. For the other seven accounts, personal interviews, Henry G., 2000, Alan N., 2001; PCN 641059 (Louis F., 1998), PCN 605790 (David M., 1996), PCN 16648 (Emil N., 1996), PCN 635867 (Morris P., 1998), VHF; T-955 (Guta T., 1987), FA. According to Guta T. as well as Pola F., the Ukrainian guard had been bribed to permit the escape. RG-1383 (Pola F., 1986), MJH.

33. M-49/1172 (Mendel K., 1945), YVA.

34. M-49E/1742 (Lena W., 1946), YVA.

35. Personal interview, Henry G., 2000.

36. In addition to Lena W. and Mendel K. cited above, Becker, pp. 648 (Leo B., 1966), 826 (Ben Z., 1967), 861 (Eva Z., 1967), 1329 (Alan N., 1968); PCN 635519 (Harry S., 1998), VHF; personal interview, Alan N., 2001. As usual, at least one witness remembers a different person and names the "Silesian" (Schleser) rather than Schroth as the one responsible for throwing the hand grenade. Becker, p. 640 (Henry A., 1966).

37. Becker, pp. 437 (Toby Wo., 1966), 755 (Leonia F., 1966).

38. M-49/1172 (Mendel K., 1945), YVA; Kalman E., 1946, in

Niewyk, *Fresh Wounds*, p. 93; Becker, pp. 738 (Toby We., 1966), 775 (Leonia F., 1966), 1375 (Jankiel C., 1968); T-1884 (Regina N., 1992), FA.

39. Becker, pp. 733, 1329 (Alan N., 1967 and 1968).

40. Personal interviews, Henry G., 2000, and Howard C., 2001; Becker, pp. 715 (Ida G., 1967), 726 (Bella W., 1967), 1365 (Rachel P., 1968).

41. Becker, p. 470 (Adam G., 1966); T-1884 (Regina N., 1991), FA.

42. Becker, p. 715 (Ida G., 1967).

43. Becker, p. 654 (Mayer G., 1966).

44. Becker, pp. 23 (Mach A., 1962), 30 (Israel A., 1962), 80 (Pinchas H., 1962), 95 (Zvi U., 1962), 648 (Leo B., 1966), 715 (Ida G., 1967), 742 (Mendel T., 1966), 1365 (Rachel P., 1968), 1369 (Max R., 1968), 1416 (Akiva R., 1968); O-2/319 (Moses W., n.d.), M-49/1172 (Mendel K., 1945), M-1/E.2469 (Josef K., 1948); RG-1984 (Regina N., 1988), MJH. The brothers Israel and Mach A., Mendel T., and Joseph K. credited the speech to Becker, not Baumgarten. Three witnesses gave different versions of the death of Moshe Herblum. According to two, he was left to die a slow, painful death. Becker, pp. 430 (Hersz T., 1966), 1375 (Jankiel C., 1968). According to another, he slit his wrists. Becker, p. 726 (Bella W., 1967).

45. Becker, p. 462 (Annie G., 1966).

46. Becker, p. 95 (Zvi U., 1962); M-49/1172 (Mendel K., 1945); M-1/E.2469 (Josef K., 1948); O 2/319 (Moses W., n.d.), YVA; Niewyk, *Fresh Wounds*, p. 93 (Kalman E., 1946).

47. Becker, p. 1329 (Alan N., 1968); personal interview, Alan N., 2000.

48. Becker, p. 1937 (Salamon B., 1968); PCN 17158 (Paul C., 1995), VHF.

49. For one group, see PCN 641059 (Louis F., 1995), VHF. For a group of ten, including Abraham Wilczek, personal interview, Anna W., 2001.

50. Becker, p. 85 (Mendel M., 1962); personal interviews, Anna W., Alan N., and Howard C., 2001.

51. Becker, p. 635 (Mania B., 1966); personal interview, Regina N., 2001; PCN 5829 (Irene H., 1995), VHF; Kalib, *The Last Selection*, p. 212.

52. Becker, p. 866 (Anna W., 1967).

53. Becker, pp. 80 (Pinchas H., 1962), 95 (Zvi U., 1962), 733 (Alan N., 1967); PCN 5829 (Irene H., 1998), PCN 640106 (Rachel P., 1998), VHF; O-3/8489 (Chaim G., 1995), YVA; Niewyk, *Fresh Wounds*, p. 93 (Kalman E., 1946).

54. RG-1383 (Pola F., 1986), MJH; PCN 17158 (Paul C., 1995), VHF; M-49/1172 (Mendel K., 1945), YVA. These three accounts differ as to exactly when and for how long the Lagerrat members were under watch.

55. PCN 641059 (Louis F., 1998), VHF.

56. For Friday, July 28, 1944, as the date of the evacuation of the camp, see Becker, p. 80 (Pinchas H., 1962); personal interviews, Martin B. and Howard C., 2001; Kalib, *The Last Selection*, p. 213.

57. Becker, pp. 80 (Pinchas H., 1962), 95 (Zvi U., 1962).

58. PCN 640106 (Rachel P., 1998), VHF.

59. Becker, p. 23 (Mach A., 1962).

60. Becker, pp. 1365 (Rachel P., 1968), 1370 (Max R., 1968).

61. Becker, pp. 767 (Howard C., 1966), 839 (Zelda W., 1967).

62. M-1/E.2469 (Josef K., 1948), YVA.

63. For Kolditz, Becker, p. 409 (Fred B., 1966).

64. Personal interview, Anna W., 2001; Becker, p. 870 (Anna W., 1967).

65. Becker, pp. 591 (Maurice W., 1966), 643 (Henry A., 1966), 1370 (Max R., 1968); PCN 18549 (Saul M., 1996), PCN 600447 (Chaim W., 1997), VHF. Only one male survivor of the closed cars stated that his car was not overfilled and carried only eighty prisoners. Becker, p. 416 (Matys F., 1966).

66. Becker, p. 649 (Leo B., 1966).

67. Personal interview, Howard C., 2001.

68. Becker, pp. 635 (Mania B., 1966), 819 (Faye G., 1967).

69. Becker, pp. 511 (Dina T., 1966), 760 (Mina B., 1966).

70. T-955 (Guta T., 1987), FA.

71. Personal interview, Anna W., 2001.

72. Becker, pp. 409 (Fred B., 1966), 494 (Ralph C., 1966), 506 (Mayer S., 1966), 649 (Leo B., 1966), 787 (Max N., 1967), 827–8 (Ben Z., 1967).

73. O-3/9394 (Ruben Z., 1996), YVA.

74. Becker, p. 591 (Maurice W., 1966).

75. Becker, p. 643 (Henry A., 1966).

76. M-1/E.2469 (Josef K., 1948), YVA.

77. M-49/1172 (Mendel K., 1945), YVA.

78. Becker, p. 416 (Matys F., 1966).

79. Becker, p. 430 (Hersz T., 1966).

80. Becker, p. 511 (Dina T., 1966).

81. Becker, p. 518 (Ruth W., 1966).

82. Becker, pp. 655–56 (Mayer G., 1966). Mayer G., however, gave the name of Kogut instead of Wilczek.

83. Becker, p. 728 (Bella W., 1967).

84. Becker, p. 742–43 (Mendel T., 1966).

85. Becker, pp. 648 (Leo B., 1966), 717 (Ida G., 1967), 728 (Ryka S., 1967), 815 (Alter W., 1967).

86. Becker, pp. 827 (Ben Z., 1967), 870 (Anna W., 1967). Ben Z. stated explicitly that he had wanted to get into the first car, having heard the rumor that the camp council had arranged to be freed by the underground, but he then reconsidered for two reasons. He feared getting caught in a shootout and the car was so crowded that struggles had already broken out for places near the windows.

87. Becker, pp. 787 (Max N., 1967), 819 (Faye G., 1967).

88. Becker, p. 833 (Ben L., 1967).

89. T-1884 (Regina N., 1991 and 1992), FA.

90. Kalib, *The Last Selection,* p. 220.

91. Those specifically identifying the victims as Jewish council and police members: PCN 633693 (Rachel A., 1997), PCN 5829 (Irene H., sister of Szachter Kalib, 1995), PCN 634090 (Toby K., 1997), PCN 16648 (Emil N.,1996), PCN 620109 (Tova P., 1998), VHF. Those who just mentioned killing: PCN 20498 (Leon M., 1996), PCN 23509 (Anita T., 1996), VHF. One testimony specifically confirmed that the killers were Jews transferred from a camp further east, who were angry with the camp leaders. Henry K. (1996), UMD.

92. Personal interviews, Regina N. and Emil N., 1997; Henry G., 2000; Alan N., Howard C., and Harry C., 2001.

93. For testimony of the children and the weak coming into the camp, see Kalib, *The Last Selection,* p. 220; PCN 633693 (Rachel A., 1997), PCN 629188 (Esther K., 1997), PCN 634090 (Toby K., 1997), PCN 5829 (Irene H., 1995), PCN 20498 (Leon M., 1996), VHF; personal interview, Martin B., 2001. For others who testified that there was no selection, M49E/1669 (Leon W., early but n.d.), O 2/319 (Moses W., n.d.), O-3/9394 (Ruben Z., 1996), YVA; RG-1383 (Pola F., 1986), MJH; personal interviews, Anna W., 2001, Chris L., 2001, Alan N., 2001, Howard C., 2001; PCN 635637 (Salek B., 1998), PCN 18549 (Saul M., 1996), PCN 635519 (Harry S., 1998), VHF.

94. PCN 634090 (Toby K., 1997), VHF.

95. Personal interview, Martin B., 2001.

96. Becker, pp. 373 (Chaim R., 1966), 462 (Annie G., 1966); PCN 614515 (Ruth K., 1996), PCN 600447 (Chaim W., 1997), VHF; T-1884 (Regina N., 1992), FA.

97. T-955 (Guta T., 1987), FA; PCN 633693 (Rachel A., 1997), VHF.

98. For selection with Mengele, T-91 (Israel A., 1980), FA; personal interview, Henry G., 2001; PCN 17158 (Paul C., 1995), PCN 16648 (Emil N., 1996), PCN 640106 (Rachel P., 1998), PCN 23509 (Anita T., 1995), PCN 14818 (Joseph Z., 1995), VHF. For selection without mention of Mengele, T-1683 (Meyer K., 1988), T-442 (Sarah W., 1983), FA; PCN 19958 (Miriam M., 1995), VHF. For mention of Mengele but no selection due to the intervention of Baumgarten, T-1884 (Regina N., 1992), FA; PCN 633693 (Rachel A., 1997). For mention of Mengele and selection, despite the Baumgarten letter, PCN 600447 (Chaim W., 1997), VHF.

99. RG-50.030*250 (Guta B. W., 1990), USHMM.

100. M-1/E.2469 (Josef K., 1948), YVA.

101. PCN 605790 (David M., 1996), PCN 19958 (Miriam M., 1995), PCN 20498 (Leon M., 1996), PCN 620109 (Tova P., 1998), PCN 23509 (Anita T., 1995), PCN 600447 (Chaim W., 1997), VHF.

GEORGE L. MOSSE SERIES
IN MODERN EUROPEAN CULTURAL AND
INTELLECTUAL HISTORY

Series Editors

Stanley G. Payne, David J. Sorkin, and John S. Tortorice

Collected Memories: Holocaust History and Postwar Testimony
Christopher R. Browning

Nazi Culture: Intellectual, Cultural, and Social Life in the Third Reich
George L. Mosse

What History Tells: George L. Mosse and the Culture of Modern Europe
Stanley G. Payne, David J. Sorkin, and John S. Tortorice